How We Can Halt
Inflation and
Still Keep Our Jobs

How We Can Halt Inflation and Still Keep Our Jobs

WILLIAM W. TONGUE

 1974

DOW JONES–IRWIN, INC.
Homewood, Illinois 60430

First Printing, October 1974

Library of Congress Cataloging in Publication Data

Tongue, William, 1915–
    How we can halt inflation—and still keep our jobs.

    1. Wage-price policy—United States. 2. Wage-price
policy—Europe. I. Title.
HC110.W24T66   331.2'1   74–12932
ISBN 0-87094-087-2

Printed in the United States of America

To Beve

Preface

THIS BOOK stems from a growing disillusionment and dissatisfaction over the failure of traditional monetary and fiscal policy tools, by themselves, to deal adequately with inflation. We as citizens should be satisfied with nothing less than full employment *and* stable prices. The answer to attaining these goals could include an element of "incomes policy," as the Europeans call it, or direct control of income settlements. I do, in fact, conclude that a form of incomes policy should be a permanent adjunct to adequate monetary and fiscal policy in the anti-inflation kit of tools. I leave it to the reader to judge for himself the adequacy of the reasoning and supporting evidence.

The preparation of this book was made possible by a sabbatical leave from the University of Illinois at Chicago Circle during the academic year 1971–72, for which I am most grateful. The leave permitted travel and interviewing in Western Europe on the place of incomes policy in the strategy of inflation control.

Thanks are due to many people who arranged interviews for me or were kind enough to discuss their own work or activities in the area of incomes policy and inflation control. In the United States these included Walter E. Hoadley of Bank of America, Frank W. Schiff of the Committee for Economic Development, Harold C. Passer who was Assistant Secretary of Commerce, M. P. Venema of Universal Oil Products Company, Henri de Voguë of William Blair and Company, and Hans A. Widenmann of Loeb, Rhodes and Company. Over a longer period, I believe I gained most from reading and conversing on the subject with four former chairmen of the Council of Economic Advisers: Gardner Ackley, Walter W. Heller, Paul W. McCracken, and Raymond J. Saulnier. Discerning readers will recognize the similarity of my views to those of Gardner Ackley, though I absolve him of all responsibility.

A great many people assisted me in Europe. From Norway, I am especially grateful to Odd Aukrust of the Central Bureau of Statistics and chairman of the fact finding committee for the income settlements; Hermod Skänland, director of the Bank of Norway; Messrs. Bakke, Oien, and Skipeness of the ministry of Prices and Wages; and to Thor Bang and Axel Dammann of Den Norske Creditbank. In Sweden, I am indebted to Erik Dahmen of the Stockholm School of Economics and Stockholms Enskilda Bank, and to Torsten Carlsson and Bengt Gronquist of Skandinaviska Banken. I received kind help in England from Sir Douglas Allen and D. W. G. Wass of Her Majesty's Treasury Department,

R. J. Ball of the London Graduate School of Business
Studies, Geoffrey Bell of Schroeder Wagg & Co., David
Lea of the Trades Union Congress, Derek Robinson of
Oxford University, Tad Rybcynski of Rothschild Broth-
ers, and G. D. N. Worswick of the National Institute of
Economic and Social Research. Very special thanks are
due to Lord and Lady Robens, and to A. E. Richards and
H. R. Brooker of Universal-Matthey Products Limited,
for arranging a dinner and far-reaching discussion with
Arthur Earle of the London Graduate School of Business
Studies, Benjamin Roberts of the London School of Eco-
nomics, and Victor Feather of the Trades Union Congress.

On the continent I had rewarding conversations with
Henrik Henriques of Copenhagen and, in Holland, with
Samuel and Constant van Eeghen of Oyens & van
Eeghen N.V., P. J. de Rijke and Dr. Ruiting of the
Amsterdam-Rotterdam Bank N.V., and Prof. dr G. A.
Kessler and Drs. H. H. van Wijk of De Nederlandsche
Bank N.V.; in Germany with Dr. Helmut Schlesinger
of Der Deutschen Bundesbank and Dr. Franz-Josef
Trouvain of the Deutsche Bank AG; in Switzerland with
F. E. Aschinger of Swiss Bank Corporation, W. Kull and
John Ladermann of Swiss National Bank, and Hans Mast
of Swiss Credit Bank.

Some of the difficult social as well as political problems
associated with incomes policies are encountered in
France. I am indebted for helpful discussions to Pierre
Berger of the Banque de France, Claude Pierre-Bros-
solette of the Ministry of Economics and Finance,
J. C. R. Dow of the Organization for Economic Co-
operation and Development, James W. MacDonald of
Procofrance, Leonard Rist and J. P. Sallé of the Interna-

tional Monetary Fund, and Thierry de Voguë of the Banque de Paris et des Pays-Bas.

Thanks are due also to Sarah Seaton, Rita Bell, and Louise Malek who helped with the typing.

Last, but far from least, I would like to express my appreciation to my wife, Beve, who accompanied me on my travels and turned them into a delightful adventure and who urged me on with the writing until it was finished.

September 1974   WILLIAM W. TONGUE

Contents

1

Introduction

THE Employment Act of 1946 declares that it shall be
the policy of the United States ". . . to promote maximum employment, production and purchasing power."[1]
This has come to mean that public policy should be aimed
to achieve simultaneously the twin goals of full employment with reasonably stable prices, although the price
level objective as such was not specifically stated in the
Act. We will assume in what follows that these are still
the overriding objectives of economic policy.

The Employment Act was enacted against a background of widespread fear that without the stimulation
of wartime demands the economy would slip back into
the depression and stagnation that characterized the
1930s. Private enterprise was believed to have run out

---

[1] Footnotes are located at the end of the book.

1

of gas. The frontier was gone geographically, and industrially also in the sense that there were no innovations to be exploited, such as automobiles in the 1920s. Population growth had dropped drastically. It was widely concluded that there was little left for the economy to do but stagnate.

More than a quarter century of experience under the Employment Act has demonstrated that these fears were groundless. Not that the record has been perfect—for the economy has at times displayed annoying tendencies to cumulate to excess in both directions once it starts moving and, at other times, to languish on dead center.

Examples of excessive boom, in addition to the Korean War strains of 1950–51, occurred in 1948, 1956–57, 1968–69 and 1973, the boomiest of all in prices. The postwar record was also marred by 5 business recessions: in 1949, 1953–54, 1957–58, 1960–61, and 1970–71. The 1970–71 episode was induced deliberately, though in extent it proceeded well beyond the intentions of the engineers and the economy lagged noticeably in the early part of the recovery. Another period of stubborn lethargy occurred in the early 1960s.

Thus, one must admit that in the postwar years the economy has operated at levels which departed most of the time from what one might conceive of as an ideal rate of activity. Nevertheless, compared with its performance prior to World War II, the postwar record has been a good one from the standpoint of providing high levels of employment and production. In the worst of the postwar recessions—1957–58—unemployment peaked at 7½ percent of the labor force in July 1958,[2] which compared with rates averaging above 20 percent in each of the years 1932 through 1935.[3]

The postwar record of a generation without a major depression or financial collapse was unique and offers ample proof that the lessons of the Great Depression were learned well. For out of that experience came developments which led to better economic understanding and to adoption of the so-called "built-in stabilizers." In the financial field these include deposit insurance and abolition of the gold standard as the basis of reserves of the banking system. On the side of income maintenance, we have unemployment insurance; social security; and a high sensitivity of federal revenues to changes in economic conditions, which tends to dampen economic expansions and cushion declines.

The market system of the United States thus shows today automatic tendencies toward stability of employment and income. In addition, through Federal Reserve monetary policy together with actions on government expenditures and taxes, it is possible to influence the course of the economy deliberately. Unfortunately, the science of economic forecasting has not yet progressed to the point where we can "fine tune" the economy so that it grows just fast enough to absorb the growing labor force, no more and no less. The recent boom excesses of 1968–69 and 1973, and the too-deep and too-long recession of 1970–71, are testimony enough to that. Nevertheless, our experience suggests that we have learned enough about guiding the economy, and have demonstrated sufficiently that the tools do work, to argue conclusively that our economic future is in fact in our own hands and need not be ruled by the unseen hand of destiny which forces us this way or that whether we will or no.

We should note that the record of our friends across

the seas—in Western Europe, Japan, and Australia-New Zealand—is even better than our own from the standpoint of maintaining high levels of employment opportunities. Parenthetically, we might observe that this record of the Western economies as a group is undoubtedly an important reason why the market system has more than held its own in the postwar years as a system of economic organization in competition with systems which rely on detailed planning of specific activities.

THE INFLATION VIRUS

Before we allow ourselves to be carried away in rapturous praise of the postwar market system, however, we must recognize that it has gradually but persistently developed a malignancy which has been growing larger and larger and which, unless brought under control, or better eradicated, threatens to overcome the good that has been accomplished in the postwar years in regularizing employment and production. The malignancy is inflation, which has plagued our economy increasingly in recent years to the bafflement of all the economic doctors. As James Tobin put it in his Presidential address to the American Economic Association in December 1971: ". . . the economy has an inflationary bias: When labor markets provide as many jobs as there are willing workers, there is inflation, perhaps accelerating inflation. Why?"[4]

One might add that inflationary bias is present even when labor markets do not provide as many jobs as there are willing workers. The 1971 experience up to the time of the August price freeze was all too vivid an example. Unemployment averaged nearly 6 percent of the labor force in the first half of 1971, but prices for the private economy rose at the annual rate of nearly 5½ percent.[5]

Clearly, the inflationary bias in our economy did not come about because anyone consciously desired it. Probably no one could be found who would be in favor of rising prices as such, though some might accept a rising price level if it would bring offsetting benefits, such as lower unemployment for example—and James Tobin might be included in that group. But, given the choice on the merits of the case itself, ignoring any incidental accompaniments—"other things being equal," as the economists say—most people would choose stable over rising prices.

THE OBJECTION TO RISING PRICES

Why do people oppose rising prices? Some do so on grounds of equity. Rising prices discriminate against those with relatively fixed nominal incomes, such as retired people (and, at one time and now possibly again, school teachers). Strictly speaking, the argument as to equity would apply only to *unanticipated* inflation. If inflation were correctly anticipated by everyone, future payments would be adjusted to that prospect. For example, interest rates jumped in 1969–70 and 1973 in part because inflation was anticipated for the future. Lenders demanded 9 percent and even 10 percent rather than 7 percent because they expected the dollars they loaned to be worth less when they would be repaid, and borrowers were willing to pay the higher rates for the same reason. The extra payment offset at least in part the costs of inflation to the lender, and took away part of the expected gain to the borrower from paying back in dollars of cheaper purchasing power. And so it is with other things.

In theory, therefore, it shouldn't make any difference what the rate of inflation is so long as it is perfectly anticipated. But in practice, once inflation gets started, it becomes very uncertain just how far and how long it will go. This uncertainty makes it extremely difficult to formulate stable plans for the future. Trying to hedge against the uncertainty of developments leads to speculative activities and to frustrations and disappointments which are not conducive to the orderly development of a stable society.

The sensitivity of the public's attitude toward business enterprise to changes in the rate of unemployment is illustrated in Table 1.

The table indicates that approval of business rises as the unemployment rate declines, and falls when the unemployment rate rises. An apparent exception occurred in 1969. Unemployment in that year was lower

TABLE 1
Public Attitude Toward Business vs. Unemployment

	Percent of Public Expressing Moderate to High Opinion of Business	Unemployment as Percent of Labor Force
1959	44%	5.4%
1961	42	6.7
1963	45	5.6
1965	51	4.5
1967	52	3.8
1969	41	3.5
1971	38	5.9

Sources: "Trends in Public Attitudes Toward Business and the Free Enterprise System," by Thomas W. Benham, President, Opinion Research Corporation, February 7, 1972, p. 4, for public opinion of business; *Economic Report of the President*, January 1972, p. 220, for unemployment figures.

than for any other year in the table; yet the percentage of the public expressing a favorable opinion toward the business establishment was lower than for any other year included in the table with the exception of 1971. A probable explanation is the fact that in 1969 the Consumer Price Index recorded a rise of 6.1 percent from December 1968 to December 1969, the highest yearly increase since the early days of the Korean War. The year 1971 combined high unemployment with a continued rise in prices until the freeze; at the same time a lower proportion of the public expressed approval of business.

Thus the business community, and all citizens concerned about stability of the social and economic order, have a significant stake in seeing to it that public and private policies are directed to the achievement of both objectives of the Employment Act of 1946: full employment *and* a stable price level. It is the purpose of this book to explore the nature and causes of the inflation that plagues us and to suggest a prescription for its cure. We conclude that solving the inflation problem will not be easy or quick. After all, we have tried to control inflation by deliberately restraining business activity—by provoking recession, unemployment, and falling profits—and by direct control of prices and of wage and salary incomes. All approaches have had little more than a transitory impact on the stubborn forward march of inflation, either in the United States or abroad.

We conclude finally, however, that the situation is not without hope. Our society can achieve both full employment and stability of prices. But mere control of demand through monetary and fiscal policy, while a necessary condition for stability of prices, is not enough given the constraints of our social and economic institutions, particularly those relating to collective bargaining. In addition, we will need some form of permanent direct controls over wage and salary incomes—an "incomes policy" as it is known in Europe—which will have sufficient teeth to be effective in preventing a price-incomes spiral; at the same time, it must be sufficiently flexible to allow the price system to play its role of adjusting relative demands and outputs of individual commodities and services to each other so as to maximize *real* incomes and satisfactions. This latter function, as a practical matter, can only be performed by the market price system in economies as complex as those of the western free world.

At this point we wish to make it clear that we look upon incomes policy as a necessary *supplement* to appropriate monetary and fiscal policies; *not* as a *substitute* for these broad, general instruments of control. Sufficient monetary and fiscal expansion is necessary for the growth of the economy. Likewise, restraint in expansion in the monetary and fiscal areas is necessary if inflation is to be controlled. But restraint in monetary and fiscal expansion is not enough, by itself, to prevent inflation, at least short of creating a socially and politically intolerable degree of economic depression and unemployment for an unbearable length of time.

We will argue that with an appropriate incomes policy the economy can be guided by monetary and fiscal policies to higher rates of employment, or lower rates of unemployment, than have been seen in recent years while still keeping inflation under control. That is what we mean when we say that monetary and fiscal policy are necessary but not sufficient to control inflation. In addition, we need direct restraint of incomes if we are to stop inflation and still keep our jobs.

2

Unemployment and Prices: The Phillips Curve

IT IS ironic that the major concern of the Employment Act of 1946, i.e., achieving and maintaining full employment, has turned out to be relatively easy of accomplishment, at least to the extent of avoiding the continued mass unemployment of the 1930s, while the problem of controlling inflation, scarcely alluded to in the Act, has become increasingly difficult, defying a solution up to now. No doubt our very success in achieving a high rate of employment has contributed to the difficulty of controlling inflation, for there appears to be a trade-off relationship between the degree of employment or unemployment of the labor force and the rate of price change. The higher the rate of unemployment, the lower the rate of inflation and, conversely, the lower the rate of unemployment, the higher the rate of inflation. It will be well to go into the nature of this relationship in some detail as it is the cornerstone of most policies designed to achieve a balance acceptable to the public between full employment and inflation.

THE PHILLIPS CURVE FOR THE UNITED KINGDOM

The trade-off relationship between unemployment and inflation is expressed in what is known as the Phillips curve, after A. W. Phillips who found such a relationship in the United Kingdom over the period 1861–1957. Phillips expressed it as a relationship between unemployment and the rate of change of wages rather than of prices. However, as we shall see more clearly later, there is a close connection between changes in wages and changes in prices. His findings can be illustrated by Figure 1.[6]

In Figure 1 the annual percentage change in money wage rates is arrayed along the vertical axis of the diagram, ranging from a rate of 10 percent at the top to −2 percent at the bottom. The unemployment rate is

FIGURE 1

Percentage Change in Money Wage Rates

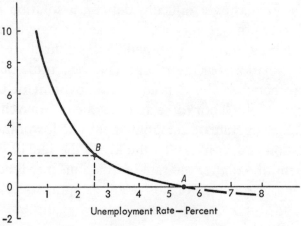

Unemployment Rate—Percent

shown along the horizontal axis and ranges up to 8 percent. The curved line is the Phillips Curve. It expresses the relationship that exists between any rate of unemployment and the rate of wage change that would normally be associated with it. For example, Point *A* in Figure 1 indicates that with unemployment of about 5½ percent the rate of change in wage rates would normally be about zero. Point *B* indicates that with an unemployment rate of about 2½ percent the annual change in wage rates would be about 2 percent.

Translated into price changes, a rise in wage rates of 2 percent per annum would be compatible with a stable price level under British conditions where output per man-hour (i.e., output per person per hour of work) has shown an increase over long periods of about 2 percent per year. Stated somewhat differently, a rise in output per man-hour of 2 percent will make possible a rise in wage rates per hour of 2 percent without an increase in prices.

These were Phillips's findings based on data from 1861 to 1913 for the United Kingdom. He also found, however, that the relationship was relatively the same whether one took the period of the late 19th century, the post-World War II years, or a period in between. That is, for England, a 5 percent rate of unemployment would be associated with the same rate of price change (and wage change) in the 1950s as in the 1860s. His postwar data, however, went only through 1956, and there may have been a change since.

THE PHILLIPS CURVE IN THE U.S.

If we could only translate Phillips's findings to the United States it would be a most happy solution to the problem of reconciling full employment with a stable price level. For 2 percent unemployment would barely cover the frictional unemployment of time between jobs, or of people coming into the labor force for the first time and searching for a suitable job. It would include very little hardship unemployment or long-term unemployment. But, sad to relate, the Phillips findings are just not applicable to the United States today. Unemployment in the United States has been well above 2½ percent of the labor force ever since the end of the Korean War, and there hasn't been a single year since then in which the general price level has failed to rise.

Part of the difference in the relationship between unemployment rates and inflation in the U.S. as against the U.K. is caused by a conceptual difference in the definition of unemployment. But the difference seems to go well beyond differences of definition. A recent estimate of the relationship for the United States by Otto Eckstein and Roger Brinner puts it as shown in Figure 2.[7] Note that in this version we show the change in prices rather than wage rates on the vertical axis.

The Eckstein-Brinner formulation is based on U.S. data from 1955 through 1970. It says that to achieve price stability would require continuing unemployment of about 8 percent, while reducing unemployment below 4½ percent would bring on an explosive inflation in prices. This conclusion may be compared with the generally accepted target of 4 percent unemployment as the definition of "full" employment. If the Eckstein-Brinner estimates are correct for present conditions, they suggest that the 4 percent unemployment target is a will-of-the-wisp and that attempts to reach it would result only in an explosive inflation.

It is ironic that the 4 percent unemployment goal was announced (by the Kennedy Administration) as an "in-

FIGURE 2

Annual Percentage Change in Prices

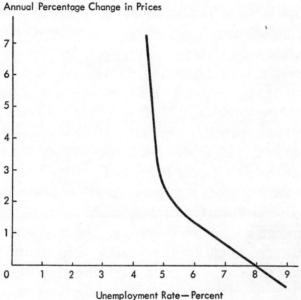

Unemployment Rate—Percent

terim" target as recently as 1962. As stated then, the goal was to be moved steadily to successively lower rates as manpower training and other measures acted to reduce "structural" unemployment.[8] Not only did the improvement in the trade-off not occur as expected, despite substantial expansion of manpower programs and the introduction of wage-price guideposts, but the trade-off apparently worsened as the decade wore on and became still worse in the early 1970s despite various degrees of wage-price controls. This is a discouraging fact, but one we must keep in mind and face up to in our further analysis.

We will pause at this point to consider a rather esoteric feature of the Phillips curves as drawn so far. They are long-run curves, to use the economists' jargon. They purport to show the effect of all the forces bearing on the inflation-unemployment trade-off, after they have had time to work themselves out fully. For example, the curve implies that if the economy could be "fine-tuned" to operate at 8 percent unemployment continuously and indefinitely, then the rate of inflation would ultimately settle near zero and stay there, though it might not go there immediately. Similarly, at a long-run level of 5½ percent unemployment, the price level would ultimately settle down to an annual rise in the vicinity of 1½ to 2 percent, year after year indefinitely.

For short periods, however, or in the "short run," a given change in unemployment would have a much more modest impact on price change. The resulting short-period curve would be much flatter, as in Figure 3. The reason is that a change in demand (for which the unemployment rate is a proxy) works its effects on prices only with a lag distributed over time.

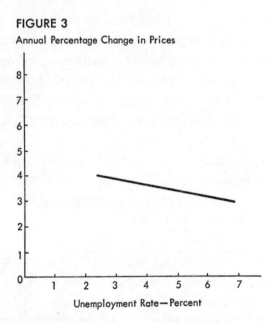

FIGURE 3

Annual Percentage Change in Prices

Unemployment Rate—Percent

If we think of Figure 3 as representing conditions in 1974, for example, a rise in unemployment would have only a negligible effect in reducing the rate of inflation *in 1974,* though it would have a continuing effect in 1975 and subsequent years—in the "long run." Similarly, pumping up the economy to a substantially lower rate of unemployment, even below 4 percent, would have only a negligible impact in raising the rate of inflation *in 1974,* but the ultimate effects in raising prices could be disastrous—again in the "long run."

In other words, the lags in the relationship of price change to employment change are substantial. For example, the excessive expansion of the economy in 1967–68 did not bear fruit in the acceleration of inflation until 1969, 1970 and 1971. We should remember, also, that the expansion of 1967–68 did not look as excessive at the time as it does now in retrospect. In illustration of this, some may recall how President Johnson vented his exasperation when he learned early in December 1968 that the Federal Reserve Board had raised the discount rate. (Unemployment then was 3.4 percent, incidentally.) Similarly, the pumping up of the economy in 1972 did not seem as excessive at the time, in the short run, as it does with the benefit of hindsight following the longer-run price explosion of 1973. However, the performance in 1973 was also affected by special factors of sufficient importance to warrant discussing this whole episode separately in Chapter 8.

EXACT TRADE-OFF IS UNCERTAIN

We mention this point about the long run and the short run, about the lags between changes in the rate of unemployment and changes in the rate of price or wage change, because the fact is that no one really knows for sure where the long-run Phillips curve may lie. The path taken by the Eckstein-Brinner version, for example, is inferred from the outcome of the equations they derive from the 1955–1970 experience, which of course consists of a succession of short runs. Moreover, they include in their model a term labeled "inflation severity factor" to account for the excess of inflation in the late 1960s and 1970 over what is explained by other factors in the equations. This raises some questions. Since the late 1960s and 1970 were the only years in the 1955–70 period when inflation went beyond what is explained by the other factors (apart from a minor deviation in 1957–58), this is close to saying that the inflation of 1967–70 was excessively severe because it was excessively severe. Probably the same could be said of the period since 1970 if the Eckstein-Brinner analysis had been carried that far.

In fairness to Eckstein and Brinner, however, it should be noted that they were properly cautious about their results:

. . . the results should not be overinterpreted, of course. The historical period on which the model is based runs only from 1955 to (but not including) 1971. The inflation severity factor took on small values in the later years of the inflation of the mid-1950s, but showed large values only in the three year episode of the end of the 1960s. Thus, in some crude sense, it can be considered to be only one observation of the critical process of forming inflationary expectations.[9]

Thus, realistically, there must be considerable uncertainty over the exact location and shape of the Phillips curve under today's conditions. Nevertheless there seems to be some agreement that the curve is relatively flat for short periods, implying that the economy (and hence unemployment) can be expanded or contracted within a wide range without substantially affecting prices immediately. Also, there seems to be agreement that the curve today lies farther to the right along the horizontal scale than was true before World War II, and possibly even in the immediate postwar years, so that a given level of unemployment today is associated with a higher rate of price increase than was true previously.

Most observers also seem to agree that in the long run, after the effects of changes in the unemployment rate have had a chance to work themselves out fully (i.e., after several years), the curve is much steeper than it is in the short run. Nevertheless, most seem to believe that even in the long run there is some rate of unemployment (say, 4½ percent) above which there is a trade-off between unemployment and inflation—i.e., the higher the rate of unemployment, the lower the rate of inflation. If the unemployment rate is brought below this critical rate in the short run, and held there, it will result in the long run in an explosive rise of prices. That is what is meant when we say that the long-run curve becomes vertical at the critical unemployment rate.

IS THERE A "NATURAL" RATE OF UNEMPLOYMENT?

Although we have said that the position of the curve, especially in the long run, is rather uncertain, most students seem to agree that it has the general shape described above and shown in Figure 1. There are some, however, who go even farther and allege that the Phillips curve in the long run is vertical over its entire course, i.e., that for the long run there is a "natural" rate of unemployment which will seek to reassert itself no matter what rate of unemployment may be established by public policies in the short run. According to this extreme view, any attempt to reduce the unemployment rate below its "natural" level through expansionary public policies may be successful for a time, but in due course will lead to inflation and ultimately to an explosive inflation.

This view has been put forward most vigorously by Professor Milton Friedman of the University of Chicago—who is not a stranger to positions that some of his colleagues consider extreme. Unfortunately, Professor Friedman has not spelled out in any detail just what the "natural" rate of unemployment might be or how to go about measuring it in any practical situation. He did offer these general guides, however, in his presidential address to the American Economic Association in 1967:

The "natural rate of unemployment," in other words, is the level that would be ground out by the Walrasian system of general equilibrium equations, provided there is imbedded in them the actual structural characteristics of the labor and commodity markets, including market imperfections, stochastic (i.e., unpredictable random) variability in demands and supplies, the cost of gathering information about job vacancies and labor availabilities, the cost of mobility, and so on.[10]

In the same address Friedman also said: "Unfortunately, we have as yet devised no method to estimate accurately and readily the natural rate of . . . unemployment."[11] But he concluded succinctly: ". . . there is always a temporary trade-off between inflation and unemployment; there is no permanent trade-off."[12]

Translating this into ordinary language, there would

appear to be three factors bearing on the location of the "natural rate of unemployment," according to Friedman:

1. The "structural characteristics of the labor and commodity markets"—by which we mean simply the extent of competition or the degree of monopoly power in those markets and legislated enactments such as minimum wage rates, the Davis-Bacon Act, unemployment insurance and other welfare arrangements.
2. The cost of gathering information about job vacancies and availabilities.
3. The costs of mobility, i.e., the costs of moving from one geographic location to another, as from West Virginia to Illinois; or from one occupation to another, as from coal miner to machine operator.

We can dismiss the stochastic variability item as having only transitory effects, with little likely impact on the long-run location of the Phillips curve.

Narrowing down the factors affecting the location of the Phillips curve in this way can help us to reach a conclusion as to what might be done to improve the trade-off between unemployment and inflation. A necessary first step is to reach a judgment on just why the trade-off is as bad as it is, and also why it has apparently worsened in recent years.

Keeping to Friedman's three criteria, as we have summarized them, there would appear to have been little or no worsening over time in points 2 and 3—the costs of gathering information and the costs of mobility. In fact, given the improvements we have had in transportation and communication, to say nothing of government training and related programs, and the general rise in living standards which makes people more mobile, one would think that developments affecting these two points would have tended to improve the trade-off, thereby tending to shift the Phillips curve to the left, whatever its shape might be.

This suggests that we need to look to the first point—the structural characteristics of markets—if we are to find the root cause of the unemployment-inflation dilemma, and the reasons for its worsening in recent years. We will center our later analysis on this aspect of the subject.

In the meantime, given our present structures in the manpower and product markets, given our present costs for search and movement in the labor market, and accepting the Eckstein-Brinner estimates of the Phillips curve of the U.S. as the best available at this time, it would appear that the most likely figure for the "natural rate of unemployment," would be in the vicinity of 8 percent. This figure is not to be attributed to Friedman, however. It is approximately the rate which would create no pressures for an increase in prices according to the Eckstein-Brinner findings, suggesting that both the labor and commodity markets would be in an equilibrium at that point which could be expected to continue for some time. The corresponding unemployment-price change curve would appear as in Figure 4.

In other words, according to Friedman, the rate of price change (in the long run) is totally unaffected by policies designed to influence the unemployment rate, which in any case can only be affected temporarily, after which the unemployment rate will return to its "natural" level, though as noted above he would not necessarily estimate that level to be 8 percent. All of which is consistent with Friedman's general position, as he argues else-

FIGURE 4

Annual Percentage Change in Prices (or wages)

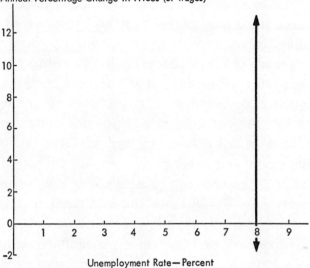

Unemployment Rate—Percent

where, that inflation is solely a monetary phenomenon.

This is not the place to debate whether Friedman is right or wrong. For regardless of whether the Phillips curve for the United States under today's conditions is a vertical straight line as Friedman envisions it (at least according to our interpretation of his statements), or is of the more generally accepted form of a trade-off relationship between inflation and unemployment, the situation remains extremely unsatisfactory. Any way we look at it, to keep prices from rising more than 2 percent per annum seems to require an unemployment rate somewhere between 5 and 8 percent, again using the Eckstein-Brinner findings. Surely this is an outcome that cannot be accepted easily by Americans. Here in the homeland of opportunity and accomplishment, we can be satisfied with nothing less than both full employment *and* stable prices!

Let us first spell out what this means in a practical sense. The existing price indexes probably have an upward bias, since they cannot fully take into account the continuing improvements in the quality of goods. This suggests that a stable price level might be consistent with an upward drift of as much as 1½ percent per annum in the consumer price index. Also, probably no one would suggest that the statistical rate of unemployment should be reduced to zero. Even in war we have had some unemployment—under 2 percent in World War II and just under 3 percent at the Korean War low for unemployment. This would mark the minimum that apparently would be needed to allow for what we usually refer to as "frictional" unemployment, meaning unemployment resulting from the fact that a person who is looking for a job may not find one just to his choice immediately, or may not be willing to incur the costs and trouble of intensifying his search or moving from one geographic location or occupation to another. An acceptable level of unemployment should contain a minimum of involuntary or hardship unemployment. Thus, in peacetime, we might settle on a target for unemployment of not more than 4 percent.

A combined target of 4 percent for unemployment and of 1½ percent for price increases should therefore be the minimum acceptable as an interim goal. Hopefully, in time we could strive to do still better. Clearly, this is not an attainable goal under present conditions as shown by studies of the Phillips curve trade-off relationship and by actual experience in the early 1970s. We must conclude that something in our institutional structure intereferes with attaining our goal of full employment without inflation, and that we will need to modify that "something" if we are to make progress toward the goal. We will come back to this.

IS 4 PERCENT UNEMPLOYMENT A REALISTIC TARGET?

It is sometimes alleged that because the labor force today contains a higher proportion of teenagers and women, and because unemployment rates are higher for these groups than for the rest of the working population, a higher overall unemployment rate should be acceptable today than in earlier times. For example, the *Economic Report of the President* for January 1972 calculates that the unemployment rate of 4.1 percent in 1956 would have been 4.5 percent if in 1956 we had had the same distribution of the labor force by age and sex as we had in 1971, assuming unemployment rates for the various groups were the same.[13]

Table 2 summarizes relevant statistics on changes in the composition of the labor force between 1956 and 1971.

TABLE 2
Civilian Labor Force, by Sex and Age, 1956 and 1971

	Thousands of Persons		Percent of Labor Force		Unemployment Rate	
	1956	*1971*	*1956*	*1971*	*1956*	*1971*
Total civilian labor force.......	66,552	84,113	100.0%	100.0%	4.1%	5.9%
Men, 20 years and over	42,658	47,861	64.1	59.9	3.4	4.4
Women, 20 years and over	19,599	28,799	29.4	34.3	4.2	5.7
Both sexes, 16–19 years......	4,296	7,453	6.5	8.8	11.1	16.9

Note: Amounts will not necessarily add to totals due to rounding.
Source: *Economic Report of the President.* January 1972, pp. 220–23.

It is true that the pressure of duties in the home may cause a woman to be less firmly attached to the labor market than a man, particularly if she is not the main breadwinner of the family, and teenagers are apt to be understandably flighty in their work preferences. But is this the major cause of their higher unemployment rate? Or is it rather that they tend to fill jobs which are somewhat marginal in nature? There have always been marginal jobs in our society, but formerly they were filled to a greater extent by men.

Granted that there may be "natural" factors making for higher rates of unemployment among women and teenagers than might be true for men holding the same jobs, there have been offsetting developments in the economy tending to reduce the susceptibility of jobs on the average to large, unexpected fluctuations. For example, the durable goods industries have long been noted for their instability of employment. These industries include manufacturing, particularly durable goods manufacturing, and mining and contract construction. But these are the very industries which have lagged in employment growth in the past 15 years. Over 90 percent of the growth in payroll employment between 1956 and 1971 occurred in the nonvolatile areas, notably trade and finance, services, and government, particularly state and local government. The relevant statistics are included in Table 3.

Thus there are factors working in both directions to affect the size of what may be termed "frictional" unemployment. On balance, there seems to be no more reason to accept a goal for unemployment above 4 percent today than there was in 1956. Besides, trying to rationalize a

TABLE 3
Wage and Salary Workers in Nonagricultural Establishments, 1956 and 1971

	Thousands of Persons		Increase	
	1956	*1971*	*Amount*	*%*
Total wage and salary workers	52,408	70,699	18,291	34.9%
Manufacturing				
Durable goods	9,834	10,590	756	7.7
Nondurable goods	7,409	8,020	611	8.2
Mining..................	822	601	221*	26.9*
Contract construction	2,999	3,259	260	8.7
Transportation and public utilities........	4,244	4,481	237	5.6
Wholesale and retail trade................	10,858	15,174	4,316	39.7
Finance, insurance, and real estate	2,429	3,800	1,371	56.4
Services.................	6,536	11,917	5,381	82.3
Government				
Federal................	2,209	2,664	455	20.6
State and local	5,069	10,194	5,125	101.1

*Decrease
Note: Amounts will not necessarily add to totals due to rounding.
Source: *Economic Report of the President.* January 1972, for 1956; U.S. Department of Commerce. *Survey of Current Business.* June 1972, pp. 5–13, for 1971.

higher target rate of unemployment smacks of saying that women and teenagers are somehow not as important as other people, i.e., as male heads of families. This surely cannot be accepted by a people dedicated to the proposition that all persons are created equal and are entitled to equal opportunity.

Women and teenagers have been given greater employment opportunities thanks in part to a reduction in the amount of needed drudgery in the home, and to some changes in people's attitudes about who should perform what drudgery there is, as well as in attitudes toward women and teenagers working. They naturally tend to move into marginal jobs previously handled by adult males. But this is no reason to argue that we should accept a standard which in effect says that certain persons are not entitled to the same treatment as others, *because* they are women or teenagers. These people may be the particular ones who have the above-average rates of unemployment at this time, but that is not a good reason to raise the target for the average itself.

Thus we have come in this chapter to at least one conclusion, even though it is negative in nature. The conclusion is that one way *not* to solve the employment-inflation tradeoff dilemma is to change the standard of what is acceptable for both unemployment and inflation. We see no reason why the standards found acceptable in the early 1960s should not be applicable today, i.e., 4 percent unemployment and 1½ percent inflation as a maximum. We recognize, however, that these objectives cannot be reached together, given today's structural economic institutions, and that for this reason some of these institutions must be changed. In the next chapter we will consider whether one of these structural economic institutions, the market price system, should be considered a candidate for modification and change.

3

The Price System

IN WESTERN societies we rely on the market price system for the organization of a large part of economic activity. Profits and the quest for profits form the heart of this system and are called on for two things: (1) to allocate society's resources to uses which will produce a maximum of satisfaction for consumers in the present, and (2) to spur the creation of new and improved products and production methods for the future. Typically, we also look to profits as a source of funds for the accumulation of productive equipment, though this is not a necessary feature of the system. We will now examine the way in which the price-profit system works to accomplish the above objectives so that we may judge the extent to which we may interfere with its operation to foster the objective of full employment without inflation.

Given the key role of profits in our economic system,

it is unfortunate that the word "profit" has acquired a negative connotation. There seems to be a feeling, especially among the young, that if something is produced for profit it is against the public interest because the profit is presumed to be extracted from the hide of the buyer, specifically the consumer. The consumer is pictured as being victimized on two counts: by being forced to pay extortionate prices on the one hand and by being forced to work at substandard wages by a greedy, grasping employer on the other. The workhouses of *Oliver Twist* come to mind. It is little wonder, though paradoxical, that young people with high motivation to advance the welfare of mankind feel guilty about helping to produce something for profit, which people are willing to pay for, and somehow feel they are performing a real service if they do something for free or for a nominal subsistence, i.e., if it is something the public is not willing to pay for.

FREE CHOICE IN THE PRICE SYSTEM

The picture of the consumer as being victimized for the benefit of profits is a far cry from reality. In truth, the consumer is not forced to buy anything or to work in any particular place. Of course, he must eat and provide clothing, shelter, and other goods and services for himself and his family. But just because he must eat doesn't mean he has to buy his food in any particular place. Numerous sellers of food vie for his family's patronage. The family is free to choose any one they like, or to go out to a hamburger place or a restaurant. Similarly with clothing, entertainment, and so on.

The consumer can pick and choose among various sellers of different goods and services, taking more of this and less of that according to his wishes and the blandishments of the different purveyors. We assume in this that he is competent to make these choices for himself or to hire an expert in areas of specialized knowledge and expertise to choose for him. This is in keeping with our general belief in freedom and is consistent with the dignity of the individual as a human being, in contrast to a dog or other animal. The individual not only may but should make these choices for himself.

Similarly, in choosing his occupation, a person is allowed wide latitude. He may accept a job in the neighborhood, move to another part of the country or to some other country, or defer his entry into the labor market in favor of obtaining more training or education. It is assumed that he will be influenced in making these choices by the money returns involved.

Money need not be the sole consideration, however. If a person prefers to work as a teacher rather than as a business executive he is perfectly free to do so. Of course, he must be willing to accept a lower remuneration for his services because the marketplace, given the general preference of people to be teachers rather than business executives, sets a higher value on business executives than it does on teachers. This is because the market values people on the basis of the contribution they can make to supplying goods and services the public wants most. Executives apparently make a bigger difference in this sense than do professors. Executive talent is scarce, and the market must pay larger amounts to keep too many individuals from becoming school teachers.

PAY AND PROFITS AS PRICE MOVERS

So money need not be the only factor influencing the choice of occupation or the area in which one chooses to live (some people prefer Florida or California to New York or Illinois). All that is needed is that the choice be influenced by money; so that, for example, increasing the pay of executives relative to the pay of professors will induce more people to become executives and fewer to become professors. Of course, the reason businesses would pay more for executives is that they feel they contribute to the profitability of the enterprise, i.e., that the presence of the executive makes possible an increase in revenues from the public which is greater than the costs associated with having the executive on the payroll. In other words, having the executive contributes to profits.

We assume further that businesses operate to maximize their profits, or at least that they will make some response to changes in the profitability of their operations. If sales and/or profits rise for some product class —economists like to talk about "widgets"—then it is expected that the production of widgets will expand, either from existing producers or, if existing producers are unable to expand or are satisfied to continue at their existing scale of operations, from other producers who move into the production of widgets. Conversely, if sales and/or profits decline in the widget industry, it is assumed that the output of widgets will also decline in due course, though possibly not immediately if the capacity to produce widgets is not easily transferable to other endeavors. Some older workers, for example, may continue on in the old building, even though younger workers may prefer to go elsewhere to modern, air-conditioned buildings, and in any case the older workers may find it not worthwhile to learn a new skill or trade. So the output of widgets may only go down gradually as old plants wear out and older workers fade away like old soldiers.

We have, then, a picture of an economy where change takes place in accordance with changes in the relative profitability of different activities. The response will likely not be perfect, and not everyone need respond. But enough producers must respond to the pull of potential profits or the push of potential losses so that expansion of output will occur in activities where profits are expected to rise and contraction of output will occur where profits are expected to fall.

We emphasize "potential" and "expected" profits because actual profits may not shift widely from the general average. For example, capital resources will flow into areas of expected greater profitability, and output will expand in these activities, while actual profits may stay close to the general average. Conversely, capital will flow out of areas of expected lowered profitability, output will decline, and this will tend to keep prices and profits in those areas from falling relative to the general average. There will thus be a tendency toward equality in the rates of profitability in different lines of activity.

Similarly, expanding areas will be able to offer higher wages and more lucrative compensation arrangements generally than areas of lower profitability, again after giving effect to personal preferences as to climate and similar factors. Some people will respond to the opportunity for monetary reward and will enter the areas of greater rather than the areas of lesser profitability. This brings about a tendency for compensation to be equalized across occupations, again giving effect to differences in personal preferences.

Profit, then, is the heart of the market system of economic organization—not in the sense that it is the sole motivating force but in the sense that it is the item of *flexibility* which enables the system to respond to changes in the relative desires of consumers or in the capacity to meet them. People may still choose to enter the teaching profession (to avoid the commercial "rat race," for example) or to locate their widget business in Florida rather than in Illinois even though the returns are lower in Florida, or to put their savings into blue chip General Motors rather than a fast-food franchise that promises a greater return but is very risky. All that is needed for the system to work is that if the public should desire more fast foods (their incomes having gone up so that they can afford the extra expense) or if technological developments should make fast foods more feasible (such as widespread automobile ownership, better roads, and improved food-preserving methods) then enough people will find it worthwhile to go into fast foods to expand the supply.

OUTPUT FOLLOWS PROFITABILITY

The way profit comes into the picture can be illustrated in terms of this fast food example. If people decide that they want more fast foods, this will increase the sales (and possibly the prices) of existing sellers of fast foods, and their profits will rise. If existing sellers of fast foods expect this to continue, they will expand and others may be attracted to the field so long as the return promised is equal to or above the returns from other lines of endeavor, again giving effect to personal preferences. This of course will expand the supply of fast foods and will keep the returns in fast foods from rising much above the general average. People will get more fast foods, which is what we postulated as their desire.

Similarly, technological developments may increase the profitability of fast foods at existing prices, through better packaging and food preservation techniques, for example, which make it possible to put up supplies of some foods centrally and distribute them to local outlets by freezer truck. The higher profits will induce existing sellers of fast foods to expand or, if they don't, the higher returns in fast foods will induce others to put their money into it rather than into something else. This will increase supplies and bring down the price, or result in added services with the fast foods—at any rate a better deal for the customer which will result in added sales at the lower price. This in turn will tend to reduce the returns in the industry to the general average, depending on the extent to which the improvement was anticipated and how rapidly demand expands. But the public will get more fast foods, and presumably less of something else where returns are lower.

PROFIT GOES WITH VALUE

Now let us look at profit in this example and ask whether it is good or bad. Is it somehow wrong for the fast food merchant to receive a profit—is it extorted from the hide of the consumer against his will? Consider that if the fast food operator is making a large profit it can only be because he is getting more from his sales to his customers than he needs to cover his expenses for rent, heat, light, power, and the good old payroll—not to forget taxes! Presumably the fast food operator must pay as much for these services, including the cost of labor, as does anyone else. After all, assuming that his business is expanding, who would work for him if he didn't at least match what others are willing to pay, again giving effect to personal preferences? Therefore, the fact that the fast food merchant is making a profit can only mean that customers are willing to pay more for this service than the cost of providing it, which they will do only if they think it is a good deal in comparison with the other things they can do with their money.

Contrast this with another service in the retail field. Grocery stores in central shopping areas are declining in number because of falling profitability. And why is this? Because customers find it more convenient to go to the newer outlying shopping centers with large, modern facilities and ample parking rather than to fight their way into the downtown area and then have to park three blocks away! Does this mean that the store operator who hangs on in the downtown area is to be considered a public benefactor because he operates at a loss, subsidizing his patrons, so to speak? On the contrary, he is keeping facilities and people operating to produce something for consumers that they are not willing to pay all the costs of: not enough to cover the rent, light, heat, taxes, power, and payroll. This can only mean that these facilities and people are producing a lower value for consumers than they could produce for consumers in some other use.

By and large, then, profitability reflects the extent to which an enterprise is satisfying the demands of consumers, or is supplying a service or product which will in turn be used to supply consumers, such as power or a machine for a factory. If profitability is high after meeting pay rates and other expenses comparable to those paid by others, this is a sign that consumers are receiving something for which they are willing to pay more than if the resources so employed were used to produce something of lower profitability. On the other hand, if profitability is low, this is a sign that the enterprise is supplying consumers with a lower value than the same resources could produce in some other use. So, in response to the pull of profit, resources tend to move into areas of better than average profit and out of areas of lower than average profit, and this matches the relative values attached by consumers to different end products. Additional resources flowing into profitable areas will produce a greater dollar value for consumers than is lost by not having those resources in areas of low profitability.

SYSTEM NOT PERFECT

We said this is the way the market system works "by and large." It doesn't work perfectly, of course. We mentioned an exception for personal preferences of people as workers, so that teachers, for example, are paid less than business executives or possibly than plumbers. This means that the average consumer would gain, at least in his own judgment, as measured by what he will pay in the market, if some of the people in teaching would move into being plumbers. But offsetting this loss to people as consumers is the gain to the teacher from the fact that he prefers to be a teacher rather than a plumber. In effect, we let the market resolve this conflict of interest. Does anyone know a better way?

There are other hindrances to the perfect working of the market system. For example, automobile manufacturing apparently takes a large organization and a large amount of capital to operate efficiently. General Motors, for example, is the most profitable enterprise in the auto industry. This suggests, assuming General Motors pays as high wages and other costs as others, that the public would gain from having more of General Motors or more General Motors Corporations in place of more of Ford, Chrysler, or American Motors. But it is not as easy to multiply General Motors Corporations as it is fast food franchises. Still, let's recognize that the public is getting a good value from General Motors, again as measured by its willingness to pay enough for General Motors' cars to enable General Motors to be more profitable than its competitors. It's just too bad that there isn't some easy way to make more General Motors corporations available rather than someone else. Perhaps we should be thankful there's at least one!

The same sort of problem exists wherever there is a limitation of supply, whether artificial or otherwise. Artificial restrictions on supply are something we can presumably do something about. For example, it would be possible to loosen limitations on entry into various occupations such as banking, legal services in certain areas, membership in unions, and the like. Presumably there are good reasons for existing restrictions, but we should recognize that they do impede the efficiency with which the market system acts to give the consumer the greatest value for his or her money.

There are other inefficiencies in the operation of the system, of which the main ones would come under the category of what economists call "externalities." The best example of "externalities" is in the field of pollution. A steel mill may pour out smoke into the air and chemical pollutants into lakes and rivers. This is a cost to society but not necessarily to the enterprise unless something is done about it. And one enterprise alone cannot solve the problem—for if it goes to the expense of controlling such pollution, the cost may be so great that it will lose business to another enterprise which doesn't choose to assume this cost. The good guys will lose out to the bad guys, so to speak.

The way to handle these inefficiencies, however, is to try to remedy them within the system and not just assume that they are inevitable byproducts of the system as such. For example, steel producers can be forced by law to share the costs of controlling pollution in that they might all be required to eliminate a certain percentage of pollutants—and this percentage can be raised as close to 100 as we wish, just as in the case of automobiles. We must recognize, however, that whatever gain we achieve in reduced pollution must be matched against the higher costs or poorer performance that reducing pollution may entail. The optimum point is not always easy to determine.

MARKET SYSTEM THE ONLY ONE PRACTICAL

Recognizing that there are imperfections in the market system, not all of which can be corrected easily, it is still true that the market system is the only conceivable one that can be used to organize the production of goods and services in modern society. This is so because of the countless decisions that would otherwise have to be made by some authority as to how much of each kind of goods or services should be produced. In the modern economy, with ever-rising standards of living, it is no longer enough to keep multiplying the production of a standard list of items that represent food, clothing and shelter. We can afford not only more of these but an ever-widening list of items that constitute a bigger variety of foods, clothing, shelter and services. The competition among materials keeps growing, so that what is made of steel today may be made better of aluminum or plastic tomorrow. Which of these should be expanded, and by how much? It is perhaps needless to go on, but the thought of setting up a bureaucracy to handle these decisions is frightening.

Fortunately, in the market system, these decisions are placed in the hands of consumers. As sketched out previously, consumers spend their incomes for different goods and services in accordance with their own judgments of what gives them the most value for their money, dollar for dollar. In this sense one might say that the market system is the only one which is philosophically attuned to the democratic way of life. In keeping with the dignity of man as a human being, it forces him to make a choice, in contrast to a dog or other animal whose choice has to be made for him. We should mention that whenever we speak of "him" we also mean "her." Our language, unfortunately, does not contain a useful list of "him and her" words.

It might be objected that while the market system is democratic in the sense that it leaves decisions as to what is to be produced and consumed in the hands of the people themselves, it weights the vote of each person by the number of dollars he has available. The higher paid, in effect, get more votes than the lower paid. This is true, but to the extent that the public feels it is unjust, it can be changed or modified through the tax laws affecting income and inheritances and by direct payments to the aged, the poor, and the sick, etc. The existing weights are not a necessary feature of the system as such. Care must be taken, of course, in making changes in the existing distribution of after-tax income, to insure that the gain from greater equality of income is balanced against the loss of efficiency which might ensue. This is important not only for the most effective allocation of existing resources, but for maintaining the incentive to create new products and improvements in existing products and ways of doing things, and for preserving the incentive to save which is the source of the accumulation of the capital stock in general.

ADDED VALUE THE SOURCE OF PROFITS

One final point should be mentioned. We have shown one reason why profits are important: in a market economy, profit is essential as the prime mover in getting an efficient allocation of resources. But beyond that, profit is, in effect, one form of the wages of capital. People are willing to pay for capital because it is productive, in the same sense that a worker is productive in using whatever skills he may possess. A simple example will help to explain why.

Most people will agree that an individual landscaper can do more landscaping with powered tools than he can without them. Therefore, he can earn a larger income by using the tools. Typically, these tools are sufficiently productive that the extra income he can earn by using them will more than pay back the cost of the tools over their useful life. This extra amount, beyond the amount needed to repay the cost of the tools, is the landscaper's profit if he owns the tools. It is his return on capital.

The landscaper may not have the money or capital to

buy the tools, and in that case he may borrow the money to buy them. He will of course pay this amount back, with interest, out of the extra amounts he can make by using the tools; and, hopefully, he will have a little something left over for himself. Alternatively, he can rent the tools and pay the rent out of the extra amounts he earns by using the tools. Again, hopefully, he will have something left over for himself. In any case, the source of the payment for the use of the tools, or capital equipment, is the extra value produced by using the tools or capital. If the tool user owns the tools himself, he will capture the entire return himself; if not, he will divide the return with those who do own the tools.

This is a simple example, but the principle is the same even in a large corporation. The worker can produce more and earn a higher income by using capital resources than he could without them, even after paying a return to the owners of the capital (which may of course include himself, though usually the capital resources are owned by others in a large corporation). The accumulation of capital resources will thus tend to raise the standard of living of wage and salary earners who use them, as well as of the capitalists who own the capital resources.

HUMAN CAPITAL

We should recognize that this relationship also applies to the skills that each person possesses himself—which we might call capital inside the skin. The difference is that we do not have an organized market in which capital inside the skin can be bought and sold, though it is present to a degree in the field of professional sports. Nevertheless, it is common knowledge that training and education not only enhance the earning power of the person trained or educated, but increase his earning power by more over his working lifetime than the cost of the education. This is a return which can be related to the cost of producing it in the same way the cost of a machine can be related to its return.

It is also true, if we make a distinction between capital inside the skin (labor power) and capital outside the skin (tools or equipment), that an increase in the quantity of one will raise the value of the other. Obviously, the more hands we have, the greater is the value of a given quantity of machines with which to use those hands. But it is equally true that the more machines we have, the greater is the value of a given number of hands. So, in general, the more capital there is, the greater is the value of a given laborer, or the greater is the value of a given quantity of labor power inside the skin. Consequently, the greater the quantity of capital, the greater the return to individual wage and salary earners and the greater the return from investing in training and education to add to labor power inside the skin. And, of course, this can come full circle: the greater the amount of capital inside the skin, or labor power, whether represented by number of persons or greater capacity per person, the greater is the return to capital in the usual sense. As an example, the more skilled machinists there are, and the more highly skilled they are, the greater will be the difference that a given quantity of machines will make in the total product and the more it will pay to invest in additional machines, as well as in machines of a more sophisticated nature.

The above is important in interpreting one fact of economic history which is at least curious. As we shall discuss at greater length later, it appears to be a fact in this country, and in the western world generally, that the distribution of income as between profits broadly conceived and wages and salaries (i.e., the return to capital outside the skin vs. the return to capital inside the skin) has not changed significantly since as far back as we have records. One possible explanation of this, and a plausible one, is that the return on investment in capital inside the skin has been kept roughly equivalent to the return on capital outside the skin. And this despite the institutional barriers to the flow of investment funds from one form of capital to the other, including the fact that much of formal education and training is socialized.

In the market system, then, there is at bottom little conceptual difference between profits on the one hand and wages or salaries on the other. Both are the return to economic capacity, and both are needed for the efficient allocation of resources to the lines of endeavor where they produce the greatest values for consumers. Both, of course, may be acquired by saving and investment as far as society is concerned, and by the individual through the same process as well as by inheritance. Ethically, is a person more entitled to the return from inheriting the brain of a genius than he is from inheriting the Ford Motor Company? The quantities involved are different, of course, but these can be taken care of through our tax system without throwing out the market system itself.

SUMMARY OF MARKET SYSTEM

This summary of the way the market system works and some of the philosophical questions associated with it seemed necessary to show that the price system is not just a scheme to enrich a few at the expense of the many, as some apparently believe, but is an efficient means to organize the human and capital resources of society for the production of goods and services most desired by the members of the society. As such, it is essential that the system be permitted to work freely and that it not be subject to arbitrary interference.

We have argued not only that the market system is an efficient organizational mechanism—really the only one conceivable in a society such as the United States today, with its modern economy offering such a multitude of choices—but that it is fully compatible with our notions of democracy and of the worth and dignity of the individual as a person. We might argue over the distribution of incomes produced by the existing distribution of ownership of human and capital resources but, in general, these should be handled through agreed-upon changes in the tax system affecting incomes and inheritances and not by interfering capriciously with the functioning of the price and market system.

Accordingly, in our search for a solution to the unemployment-inflation dilemma we will assume that any permanent solution will need to presume that the economy will operate with a freely functioning price and market system.

4

Roots of the Economy's
Inflationary Bias

THREE possibilities suggest themselves as institutional constraints which may have caused or intensified the dilemma in which we have found ourselves in recent years of too much inflation combined with too much unemployment. One is the Employment Act itself; the very success of the postwar campaign to attain more continuous full employment has itself contributed to inflation. A second possibility is the monopoly power of big business, particularly the *growing* monopoly power of business. Third is the monopoly power of labor unions to extract wage increases that push up prices. We will examine each of these possibilities in turn to see to what extent each might contribute to the problem and to its solution.

EMPLOYMENT POLICY TOO SUCCESSFUL?

To start with the first point, success of the full employment effort can be judged from Figure 5 which depicts the course of the unemployment rate from 1890 to date. It is clear that the unemployment rate in the postwar years has displayed much less variability than in the past. It is not evident, however, that it has averaged notably less. In fact, the average for the years 1946–1971 was 4.7 percent, which turns out to be exactly the same as in the years 1900–1929. Nevertheless, the unemployment rate in the postwar years, even at its worst, as in the recessions of 1958 and 1961, did not come up to levels reached in earlier moderate depressions, such as 1908 and 1913–14, and did not approach the peaks of

FIGURE 5
Percent of Civilian Labor Force Unemployed

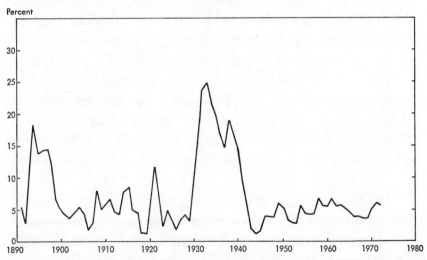

Sources: Years 1890–1928, S. Lebergott. *Manpower In Economic Growth: The American Record Since 1800.* New York: McGraw Hill, 1964, Appendix Table A-3, p. 512, for 1900–1928; Appendix Table A-15, p. 522, for 1890–99. Years 1929–1972, *Economic Report of the President.* January 1973, Table C-24, p. 220.

1921 or of the great depressions of the "Gay Nineties" and the nineteen thirties. Also, based at least on my personal observation, there has been a gradual diminution over the past 25 years of the fear that mass unemployment may return. I know of no recent incident of a Sewell Avery, the wartime head of Montgomery Ward, husbanding a hoard of cash in anticipation of a postwar depression. In this sense, at least, the old business cycle does seem to be dead.

There is no way to be certain what part the experience of lessened fluctuations in business activity may have contributed to the development of an apparently increasingly inflationary environment in the postwar years. On the one hand, one can reasonably conjecture that a lessened fear of downward fluctuations in business and profits has strengthened the businessman's resistance to cutting prices and has weakened his resistance to demands for higher wages and salaries. Similarly, in a period of soft business conditions, wage and salary workers alike will be encouraged to hold out for a job of their choosing just a bit longer if they believe business will soon turn up again than if they fear that a recession may turn into something worse. The introduction of unemployment insurance, public assistance, and social security pensions undoubtedly reinforces these tendencies. All likely have contributed to the apparent growing inflationary bias in the economy.

And yet, the case is not open and shut. The argument cuts both ways. The lessening of the threat of depression, and the income support measures for those who do become unemployed, should make employers less restrained today about separating employees than was true a generation of two ago. More to the point is the fact that in the last "New Era" before this—i.e., in the 1920s—

the attainment of full employment for a period of years (unemployment averaged only 3.2 percent from 1923 to 1929) did not set off any great fears or lead to the actuality of inflation.

Further, the rapid inflation of the years immediately following World War I did not induce an acceleration of inflationary expectations which might have carried prices and wages still higher after business turned down, despite the fact that one might have looked on that experience as merely an extension and intensification of a trend that had started back at the turn of the century, with the Consumer Price Index more than doubling between 1900 and 1920. The Consumer Price Index actually fell 16½ percent from 1920 to 1922, and then remained relatively stable through 1929.[14]

The Consumer Price Index of the 1920s left something to be desired from the standpoint of statistical purity compared with the version we use today, particularly with respect to the coverage of services. Nevertheless, the difference between the behavior of prices relative to unemployment now and in the 1920s is a difference in kind rather than merely of degree. Moreover, while the recent growing confidence in the strength of the economy may have contributed to the development of an inflationary environment, the differences from past "New Eras" do not seem so great that the very success of our full employment effort could alone account for the differences in price behavior. There must be more to it than that.

GROWTH OF MONOPOLY?

What of the power of "Big Business"? Has this increased enough in recent years to account for the persistent upward trends of the price level? The answers to these questions are not clear. It *is* clear that the largest companies have increased their share of productive activity. John M. Blair pointed out in 1966, for example, that the 200 largest manufacturing companies increased their share of value added by manufacture from 30 percent in 1947 to 41 percent in 1963.[15] Statistics compiled by *Fortune* on the top 500 industrial corporations suggest that this trend has continued at least through 1971.[16]

From this it is not conclusive, however, that there has been an increase in the power of particular firms to set prices independent of the actions of competitors in particular industries, which is what we usually mean by monopoly power. For the increase in overall concentration noted above is apparently the result of greater diversification by large firms, or greater conglomeration, rather than greater concentration of business in the hands of larger firms within particular industries. As John M. Blair also pointed out in 1966, there is no good evidence of any substantial upward movement in concentration among individual industries. For 209 industries for which concentration ratios could be calculated for both 1947 and 1963 on a comparable basis, he found:

In 43 of these 209 industries, the share held by the 4 largest producers remained relatively constant during this 16-year period, changing by less than 3 percentage points. Of the remaining 166 industries, the proportion held by the 4 largest increased in 85 and decreased in 81.[17]

Thus, it is not at all clear that the degree of concentration within industries is greater today than it was earlier on the average. Even where the concentration may have increased domestically, as with automobiles for example, the increase of foreign competition may mean that the effective degree of monopoly power has declined. Also, the range of choices open to the consumer today is so much greater than it was a generation or more ago that interproduct competition may effectively lower the degree of monopoly power of any one producer of a particular product.

In the case of materials, also, interproduct competition has intensified with the passage of time, and foreign competition is increasingly a factor. In steel, for example, not only has the dominance of U.S. Steel been reduced within the industry, but foreign competition has increased, and other materials also encroach on markets once dominated by steel—such as aluminum, plastics, and even paper. In addition, there are some industries in which the number of competitors has increased, aluminum being an example.

This is important, because only if the degree of monopoly power has *increased* would it be a factor tending to raise prices. A business firm, to the extent that it had monopoly power, should already have been using that power to the fullest extent possible to extract the maximum profit. Thus, its prices relative to costs should already have been as high as they would go in the absence of changes in other factors. Only if the degree of monopoly power increased would the monopolist have an incentive to raise prices further because only then would he increase his profits.

Finally, if the degree of monopoly power had increased over the years one would expect that the distribution of income would have altered in some way in favor of profits at the expense of wage and salary income. But there is no evidence that this in fact has occurred. Profits after taxes, for example, were $10.5 billion in 1929 or 10.2 percent of the Gross National Product of $103.1 billion in 1929. In contrast, in 1966, a peak year for profits in the past decade, profits after taxes were $49.9 billion, or only 5.8 percent of GNP.[18] For 1973, also a year of good business, profits were $72.9 billion or only 5.6 percent of GNP.[19]

So if the degree of monopoly power has in fact increased, it at least hasn't redounded to the benefit of stockholders out of proportion to the growth in overall output of goods and services. Incidentally, the figures above show just how small profits are in relation to the total value of all production; about one twentieth. Further, only 41 percent of those profits were distributed in dividends in 1973. The rest were reinvested in business expansion.

It may be argued, with justification, that the figures cited above on profits after taxes and other charges give a distorted view of what has happened to the profit share in output in the market place. It might be argued that one should look at gross profits, not net profits after taxes and other charges, since some of the latter charges are quite arbitrary in amount. Profits in this gross sense, including all charges other than employee compensation, have not changed in the postwar years as a share of the nation's gross private product or income. Such profits, or "nonlabor payments" as they are dubbed by the Department of Labor, ranged from a low of 35 percent of the nation's total gross private product in 1947 to a high of 39.5 percent in 1965. Within these limits there has been no observable tendency for the gross profit share to widen or narrow over the years. It was 36.6 percent in 1972, for example.

The fact that gross profits, in the sense of all nonlabor payments, have held a steady relationship to gross private product means that the remaining share of the product, employee compensation, has also stayed in a narrow range, actually between 60.5 percent and 65 percent. Figure 6 shows total private gross national product and employee compensation for the private economy in the postwar years. It illustrates the closeness of the relationship and the absence of any observable tendency for the gap between them to widen or narrow.

FIGURE 6
Private Gross National Product and Compensation of Employees (billions of dollars)
Billions of Dollars

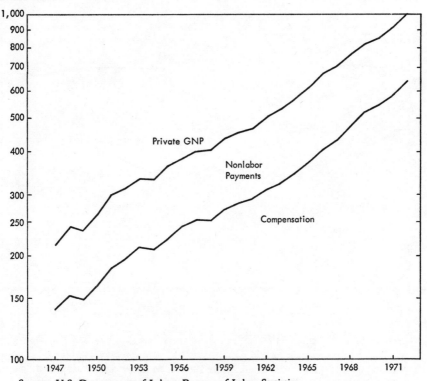

Source: U.S. Department of Labor, Bureau of Labor Statistics.

52

The astute reader will perceive from the foregoing that not only are *net* profits much smaller in relation to gross national product than gross profits or nonlabor payments, but the share of net profits in the national product has declined while the share of gross profits has not. Also, net profits have fluctuated much more widely than gross profits in response to business cycle changes. These relationships are portrayed in Figure 7.

FIGURE 7

Nonlabor Payments and Net Profits as Percent of Gross Corporate Product (excluding product originating in rest of world)

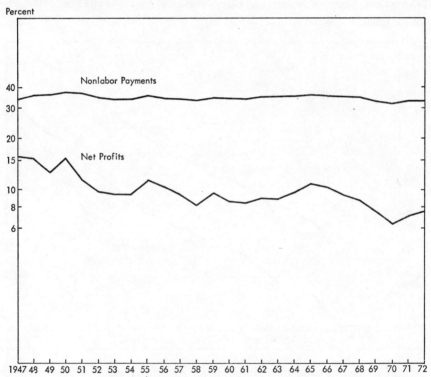

Source: U.S. Department of Commerce. *Survey of Current Business,* vol. 45, no. 9, Sept. 1965, p. 52 for 1947–1963; vol. 48, no. 7, July 1968, p. 24 for 1964 and 1965; vol. 50, no. 7, July 1970, p. 22 for 1966 and 1967; vol. 52, no. 7, July 1973, p. 23 for 1970–1972.

The reason for these divergent movements of gross and net profits is that capital consumption allowances and other nonlabor charges that lie between gross and net profits typically do not fluctuate widely from year to year, and they have trended upward in relation to the value of output in the postwar years. Illustrative statistics are shown in Table 4 for gross corporate product originating within the United States. The figures cover two years of active business conditions, 1948 and 1968, and two years of business recession, 1958 and 1970.

Parenthetically, we should observe that to the extent there may have been a profit squeeze in the postwar years, as some allege, it is not a squeeze between rising labor costs and lagging receipts. For all practical purposes, labor costs in relation to the value of output are no higher today than they were earlier in the postwar period. The squeeze has come from rising nonlabor payments relative to the value of output, notably rising depreciation allowances. However, it will not serve our purposes to go into the subject further here. We will come back to it later in another connection.

In citing these facts on profits in relation to the value of output we do not mean to defend in any way the existence of such monopoly elements as may be present in the economy. All we are trying to say here is that there is no good evidence that the degree of monopoly power has increased sufficiently in the past few generations to account for the shift in the economy to a strong inflationary bias. It is still possible, of course, that the monopoly elements on the employing side of the economy, *in combination with changes elsewhere* in the structure of the economy, may have contributed to giving the economy an inflationary bias even though the degree of monopoly

TABLE 4

Gross Corporate Product (excluding product originating in the rest of the world)

	Billions of Dollars				Percent of Total			
	1948	1958	1968	1970	1948	1958	1968	1970
Compensation of employees	91.0	163.9	319.5	369.0	64.1	66.3	64.9	67.4
Nonlabor payments (gross profits)	50.8	83.2	172.9	178.8	35.8	33.7	35.1	32.6
Capital consumption allowances	7.0	22.0	46.8	56.0	4.9	8.9	9.5	10.2
Indirect business taxes	12.5	23.7	45.5	53.1	8.8	9.6	9.2	9.7
Net interest	-.8	-1.8	.2	5.0	-.6	-.7	.0	.9
Corporate profits taxes	12.5	19.0	39.9	34.8	8.8	7.7	8.1	6.4
Net profits	21.8	20.6	43.8	34.6	15.4	8.3	8.9	6.3
Inventory valuation adjustment	-2.2	-.3	-3.2	-4.8	-1.5	-.1	-.7	-.9
Total gross corporate product	141.9	247.2	492.4	547.8	100.0	100.0	100.0	100.0

Note: Amounts will not necessarily add to totals due to rounding.
Source: U.S. Department of Commerce, *Survey of Current Business*, Vol. 45, No. 9, September 1965, p. 52 for 1948 and 1958; Vol. 52, No. 7, July 1972, p. 21 for 1968; and Vol. 53, No. 7, July 1973, p. 23 for 1970.

power may not have increased and may even have declined.

THE POWER OF LABOR UNIONS?

Our examination being at best inconclusive as to the extent to which our inflationary environment is the product (a) of our success in achieving full employment or (b) of monopoly elements in business, let us now turn to look at a third possible cause: the relation between prices and labor costs, and the connection this may have with the power of labor unions.

At the outset, let it be clear, we wholeheartedly applaud and support the *objectives* of labor organizations in trying to advance the welfare of their members. One can also commend the sentiment behind the statement in Section 6 of the Clayton Act, which exempts labor unions from the antitrust laws, that "the labor of a human being is not a commodity or article of commerce."[20] But an investigator into the issues, trying to be as objective and scientific as is possible in the social sciences, should not let such sentimental good wishes blind him to the possibility that monopoly elements in labor organizations may be more related to price changes and the inflation problem than to the welfare of the membership in particular unions or of wage earners in general.

Although wage earners or other people are not commodities in the usual sense of having a market in which they are bought and sold bodily, except perhaps in certain commercial sports activities as noted earlier, it must be recognized that the labor power possessed by a person is in effect a commodity which is bought and sold and has a market price. Also, it can be contracted for over varying periods of time ranging from an hour, a day, or a week, to several years. *In this sense* hiring labor power is no different from renting a computer, a truck, or a building. All contribute to the production process and are valued accordingly, and all belong to someone. The only difference is that a person is not allowed to sell outright the labor capacity he owns within his skin as he is allowed to sell productive capacities he may own outside his skin—or to buy those owned by others.

Let us then take a look at the facts as to the relationship between prices, on the one hand, and wages, salaries, and fringe benefit costs on the other. Figure 8 shows indexes of prices of manufactured commodities compared with an index of labor costs per unit of output for the postwar years. The index of prices of manufactured commodities is derived from the regular wholesale price index sources of the Bureau of Labor Statistics of the U.S. Department of Labor; and the index of unit labor costs is derived from the Department of Commerce estimates of wages and salaries, and supplements thereto such as social security contributions, together with the Federal Reserve Board Index of Industrial Production.

It will be seen that there is some variation in the relationship between the two series as between good years and bad over the course of the business cycle, with prices tending to be higher than average relative to labor costs in years of strong business activity and lower relative to labor costs in years of recession, such as 1949, 1954, 1958, 1961, and 1970. This is what one would expect as a matter of plain common sense. That is, in years of recession some people will be retained on the payroll even though sales and output are down, as the firm tries to hold together its key employees in anticipation that

FIGURE 8
Prices versus Unit Labor Costs of Manufactured Products (1967-100)

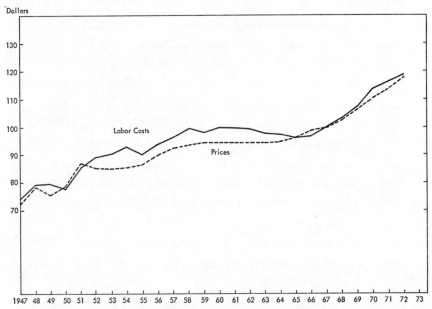

Source: U.S. Department of Commerce. *Business Conditions Digest:* July 1973 for price data through 1971 and August 1973 for unit labor costs through 1971; September 1973 for 1972 data.

business in due course will recover. At the extreme, a firm will keep *a* president (though not necessarily *the* president) if business declines, and his salary will be spread over fewer units of output—thus tending to raise costs per unit. The same will be true to a degree with vice presidents, foremen, and other key persons.

On the other hand, when business expands it is not necessary, at least at first, to expand the work force quite as rapidly, and costs per unit of output therefore tend to decline or rise less rapidly. Thus we see labor costs either declining or rising only slowly in the early periods of business recovery and then climbing in the later stages of expansion and in the early stages of contraction in business activity.

But the really striking feature of the relationship of prices to labor costs is that there seems to have been little drift in the relationship one way or the other over the years since World War II. Moreover, other data would suggest that this has been true for about as far back as we have records on manufacturing. For example, in 1899 wages and salaries amounted to 48.7 percent of value added in manufacturing (i.e., the dollar value of products less cost of materials, supplies, fuel, and electricity); some other figures along the way include 50.3 percent in 1909, 50.5 percent in 1925, and 51.1 percent in 1937. While these are merely selected at random, they are not significantly different from recent figures which are in the vicinity of 50 percent.[21]

To the extent that there may be some upward shift in the percentage in the past 70 years, this is probably due more to the change in the method of calculating value of products to obtain value added by manufacture than to any increase in the share of output going to wages and salaries. For example, since 1933 the value of contract work has been deducted from value of products to obtain value added by manufacture. This has the effect of raising the stated percentage of labor costs to value added for years since 1933 relative to that for 1933 and earlier.

What is true of manufactures also seems to be true of the economy as a whole. We saw this earlier in Figure 6, which presented the results of the recent calculations by the Department of Labor in which output for the total private economy is divided between labor compensation and nonlabor payments. Here, too, the stability of the labor share in total output is the standout feature.

It is interesting to speculate as to why the distribution of output and income between labor payments and non-labor payments (or property income in a gross sense) should have remained so nearly constant over the years despite the vast changes that have occurred in the institutions affecting labor-management relations, in the forms of taxation, and in the relative importance of different industries. It suggests that there must have been relatively constant returns to scale as output has multiplied during this century, and that therefore the relative quantities of labor and capital have maintained a rough equivalence to each other.

This last does not mean that the quantity of capital *per person* has stayed the same, for obviously capital per person has increased enormously and has been a major factor in the growth of output per person. But it would follow from the constancy of the division of output that the real quantity of labor power has kept pace with the growth of output and the growth of capital, that the growth of capital per person has been matched by the growth of labor power per person.

Stated another way, we might say that the quantity of capital inside the skin appears to have about kept pace with the quantity outside the skin. Apparently institutional changes have not been so great that forces affecting the flow of investment by society have been impeded in allocating a rough equivalence of investment between capital as we usually think of it (i.e., capital outside the skin) and capital in the sense of labor capacity (i.e., capital inside the skin). For example, although the absence of slavery makes it impractical for private investors to invest substantially in the labor power of others, society finds it worthwhile to do this through its social institutions, such as tax-supported schools and other subsidies to education and training. One must conclude that whatever the barriers may be between investment in capacity inside the skin as compared with that outside the skin, they apparently haven't changed drastically since the turn of the century.

But more important for our purposes, and irrespective of the reason, the facts indicate that there is a tight link between labor costs, profits, and prices over time. They all move together, which is the significant consideration for our analysis of whether union power is one of the causes of the inflationary bias in our economy. Unfortunately, the closeness of the relationship proves nothing as to which causes which or whether they are all jointly related to some other factor. Monetarists of the Chicago School, for example, would say that they are all related to the money supply and that all we need to do to stabilize prices and costs is to keep the money supply growing constantly at a rate equal to the rate of growth of output.

The suggestion by the monetarists that all we need to do to control prices is to control the money supply implies that both union and nonunion rates of wages and salaries respond positively and proportionately to changes in demand conditions: i.e., that when the money supply and demand increase, wages and salaries also increase to the same degree; and that when the money supply and demand increase less rapidly or decline, wages and salaries also rise less rapidly or decline. This, in effect, describes our previously discussed Friedmanesque Phillips curve of a vertical line extending up from the horizontal axis at the "natural" rate of unemployment. We recall that this Friedmanesque Phillips curve represents a long-run relationship, and that in the short run it is subject to substantial qualification for lags of uncertain duration and variability.

UNION VS. NON-UNION WAGE ADJUSTMENTS

Now whatever the long-run equilibrium situation may be—and it is unlikely that the public would ever tolerate an experiment of sufficient duration in real life to ascertain it—there is evidence from recent experience that *in the short run* wages and salaries in the nonunion sector are much more responsive to changes in demand conditions than are wages in the unionized sector. The Department of Labor has been keeping track of "effective wage adjustments" in manufacturing since 1959. In 1970 these covered 12.6 million production and related workers in manufacturing establishments that make general wage changes. Firms making adjustments on an individual basis are excluded. The effective wage adjustment is the median for all establishments with a regular adjustment policy, including those making no adjustments or having decreases, if there be any such these days. At any rate, separating this group into union and nonunion establishments makes it possible to distinguish differences in behavior in response to changes in demand conditions. Assuming changes in demand conditions are represented by the overall unemployment rate, as in the typical Phillips curve, the response of the two groups is shown in Figure 9.

The evidence here is fairly clear that a Phillips curve drawn for nonunion workers would be of the form usually expected, with a downward slope from left to right. However, a curve for the union relationships would be difficult to draw and it might be argued that the union

62

FIGURE 9
Effective Wage Adjustments in Manufacturing

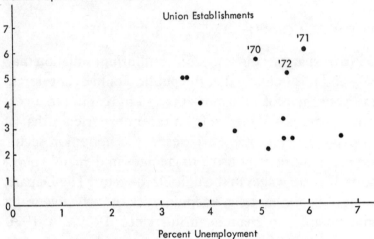

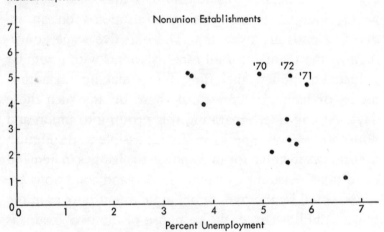

Source: U.S. Department of Labor, Bureau of Labor Statistics. *Current Wage Developments,* September 1973, p. 55, Table 3.

segment shows no relationship at all. This of course is for the manufacturing segment only. It leaves out construction and transportation where we have had some outsized settlements in recent years. We identify the years 1970, 1971, and 1972 since they seem to be on a different level than the earlier years. This also suggests that union and nonunion adjustments are not completely independent of each other.

It should be noted that the discussion above concerns *median* adjustments, which means the middle adjustment for each group in each year—i.e., half of the adjustments are higher than the median and half are lower. Since 1969 the Department of Labor has also been calculating *average* wage adjustments, which are weighted by the number of persons affected by a particular action. This substantially widens the apparent difference between union and nonunion adjustments, as reflected in Table 5.

The evidence of the unresponsiveness of union wage adjustments to changes in demand conditions ties in well with the fact of a worsening of the tradeoff between wage-price changes and unemployment in recent years compared with the situation in times past, such as the

TABLE 5

Effective Wage Adjustments in Manufacturing

	Unemployment	Median Adjustment		Average Adjustment	
	Rate	Union	Non-Union	Union	Non-Union
1969	3.5%	5.0%	5.1%	5.3%	4.6%
1970	4.9	5.7	5.1	6.4	4.7
1971	5.9	6.1	4.7	7.1	4.0
1972	5.6	5.2	5.0	5.4	4.4

Source: U.S. Department of Labor, Bureau of Labor Statistics. *Current Wage Developments,* September 1973.

1930s for example. For the percentage of the labor force represented by unions increased from 7 percent in 1930 to a peak of 25 percent in 1956.[22] The growth of union membership was especially rapid after passage of the Wagner Act in 1935. While total membership in unions reached a new high of 19.4 million in 1970, the percentage of the labor force had dropped to 22.6 percent.[23] Thus the unionized segment, while still a definite minority of the total labor force, is far stronger than it was in predepression days and is in a position to exercise strong power in particular areas to affect compensation settlements.

Some explanation of the meaning of the term "power" when applied to unions is in order at this point. Among the definitions of power carried by Webster's *New World Dictionary* is the following: ". . . great ability to do, act, or affect strongly. . . ." Thus we do not mean that the power of unions to influence wage settlements is absolute, only that it is substantial and presumably greater than the power of individual employees acting alone. This power, to the extent that it exists, is exercised in the bargaining situation between the employer and the employee and can be expected to be affected by the structure both of labor and of product markets.

Therefore, to understand the nature of union power to influence wages we need to examine the microcosm of individual labor markets in which wage bargains are set. We will do this in hypothetical fashion, keeping in mind that we wish to find an explanation of why wage changes in the union area seem to be less responsive to changes in demand conditions than they are in the nonunion area.

WAGE ADJUSTMENTS IN THE NONUNION SECTOR

Consider first a nonunion employee, say a bookkeeper in an establishment where the volume of business and the level of profits have declined. Assume that the employer would like to retain this employee even though business is down. He is considering whether to give her an increase in pay, and if so, how much.

If we think about it, we will see that his decision will be affected more by what the bookkeeper's alternatives are than by his own circumstances. For example, if business conditions are bad not only for him but also for other businesses in the labor market area, it is likely that the demand for bookkeepers will be rather slack; there may even be some unemployment among bookkeepers in the area. Under such circumstances our employer is apt to conclude that he doesn't need to give his bookkeeper as large an increase as he did in the previous payroll review. He may even be able to get by without any increase at all, figuring that the bookkeeper's chances of finding a better job are none too good, and that even if she should leave, his chances of replacing her with someone equally capable, perhaps even at a lower cost, are much better now than they were six months previously. The bookkeeper is likely to reason similarly and to be thankful for any increase she gets, probably even feeling grateful that she has a job since some of her friends are losing theirs.

Now let's look at the situation under different circumstances. Assume that the decline in business applies only to our employer. Things are pretty prosperous for others employing bookkeepers in this labor market area; orders are rising, and they are looking for more bookkeepers. Under such circumstances, bookkeepers' salaries are apt to be rising at least as rapidly as they have been in recent memory, since employers generally are anxious to keep their bookkeepers from going across the street to greener pastures—and even to attract those across the street into their own establishments.

Given these conditions our employer is apt to grant his bookkeeper an increase that will compare favorably with what others are getting, even though it may be more than the going increase was six months ago; in addition, he is apt to go out of his way to compliment her on the fine job she is doing and the important contribution she is making—not because he is a hypocrite but because circumstances make him more keenly aware of her qualities.

Since we assume the employer wants to keep this bookkeeper, he will realize that if he doesn't give her a good increase she may be hired away and that he will have a hard time replacing her. The bookkeeper for her part, if she doesn't get an increase, particularly if there is no explanation, is apt to feel slighted and probably upset. She may say to herself, "So this is the reward I get for two years of loyal service, with hardly any time off for sickness and never overstaying my coffee break, at least not more than ten minutes!" It isn't hard to see that she will find it relatively easy to switch jobs, particularly when her friends have mentioned that there are jobs open at their places.

This hypothetical but realistic look at a particuilar labor market illustrates how, in the nonunionized sector of the economy, wage changes will be rather sensitive to changes in general demand conditions, rising when demand strengthens and falling when demand weakens. Also, any one employer who finds his sales and profits dropping at a time when other businesses are prospering will likely find it difficult to keep his employees, and his operations will decline still further. Conversely, of course, someone who strikes a bonanza at a time when others are finding the going a little rough is apt to be encouraged to expand his operation, not only by the pull of demand but also by the ready availability of people and facilities.

This, parenthetically, is the way the market system is supposed to work, and does to a large extent: supplying people with the things they want (or at least are willing to pay for) rather than the things they are not willing to pay enough for to cover the costs of producing them. This is obvious in the case of the corner drugstore or supermarket, but is also true to a large extent of an American Motors or a General Electric.

So it is easy to imagine that in a world without unions it would be possible to hold the rate of wage and salary increases within bounds merely by controlling the growth of demand through general fiscal and monetary policies. Our Phillips curve under these conditions would likely be quite steep, even in the short run, rather like Professor Friedman's curve for the long run, and would lie well to the left of where it apparently is today. This implies that a small increase in unemployment would slow the rate of wage increases substantially. Since wages and prices are tied closely together, as we saw earlier, a slowdown in wage increases would also slow the rate of rise in prices. In this way, inflation could be kept under control by ordinary market forces.

WAGE ADJUSTMENTS IN THE UNIONIZED SECTOR

Now let's bring the unions into the picture. For the sake of argument, let's consider a large employer to avoid the possibility that a small employer may have special difficulty standing up to a big union. Take a food chain in a large metropolitan area, with a fleet of trucks that distribute merchandise from a central warehouse to the chain's supermarkets. The drivers of these trucks are members of the Teamsters union, as are the drivers of all other trucks belonging to food chains in the particular metropolitan area.

Now let's assume that contract expiration time is coming up and the company offers to settle with a 17½ percent increase over the next three years (about 5½ percent per year) plus some improvements in the retirement and welfare package, this being about the going rate of annual pay adjustments. Suppose then that the union says this is not enough. The union decides that it should have at least double the amount—35 percent—or it will strike.

It should be easy enough for the union to justify this demand. Probably it needs to "catch up" with some other union that received a fatter increase just after the teamsters settled last time. Also, the union may argue that the average driver doesn't earn enough to support his family, or at least to feed his children the steaks and other fine foods advertised by the supermarket chain, to clothe his children adequately for school, and to keep up the payments on the car, the TV set, and the house— which is a pretty modest one at that. All he wants is what every American wants: a little better living for his family; and he doesn't want to have to wait another three years to get it!

We can see that the union members could easily come to feel that the company offer is unworthy of consideration, that they are entitled to much more, and that the union leaders will be able to get it for them. After all, most people suffer from a dollar shortage in relation to things they would like to buy. Truck drivers in particular are a hardworking group who think the quality of their lives (or more likely their families' lives) would be much improved if they just had a few more dollars in the paycheck.

At this point we must remind ourselves that there is a physical limit to the standard of living we can attain as a nation: our ability to produce. There is no way we can eat what somebody doesn't grow, process, and transport to the supermarket. Unfortunately, our wants exceed what is available and everyone has to do without something—some people more than others, of course.

Under our system, we allocate the available supply of things by paying people for what they contribute to the general production process in the form of their labor power or the services of their property. If the total of these payments increases in line with total output, the existing volume of production will be taken off the market at relatively stable prices. If the total of incomes rises more rapidly than production, prices will rise. Since wages and salaries make up the bulk of income, and since prices and wage costs move closely together—or at least always have—this means that the rate of rise of wages and salaries in total must be kept within bounds if inflation is to be kept under control.

Now if wages and salaries in total are to be kept under control, this means that wages and salaries in specific instances must be kept on track, or that if one group gets an above-average increase, another group will have to get an offsetting below-average increase. Which brings us back to our food chain employer confronting the demand by the teamsters for a 35 percent increase. His immediate reaction is likely to be "Outrageous! We won't pay it!" But we know from experience that ultimately he will probably knuckle under and grant a large part of the union's demands. A look at this president and what is going on in his mind will help to explain why.

Some of us may think the food chain president's initial reaction to the union's demand reflects sheer cussedness and hatred for the working man. Possibly so, but probably not. Although he is probably living pretty comfortably these days, and has a good retirement program plus stock options or other tax shelters to assure him that he will be able to keep the wolf away from the door in the future, he probably remembers when he was forced to leave school and go to work to help the family after his dad had that heart attack, and how he worked during the day and went to school at night to get his degree in business administration. So he sympathizes with the teamsters and their desire for a little more.

On the other hand, he wonders what will happen to his company's competitive position if he gives in to the union. After all, there are other employees in the organization. He can't afford to pay the demands of the teamsters by cutting down the increases that would otherwise go to the other employees, for then his wage-benefit package for those employees would get out of line with the market and he would be in danger of losing his work force. Giving in to the teamsters may actually mean that increases for the other employees will have to be larger than they would be otherwise. And then—the crucial question—will his competitors go along with this? If not, his profits will be squeezed and he may find it difficult to get funds for the expansion being planned, which is to open up many new opportunities for advancement in the organization. After all, he says, profits amount to only 1½¢ on each dollar of sales, while employee costs run at least ten times that. That is why he says, "This is outrageous! We won't pay it! We'd rather take a strike of the teamsters than jeopardize the livelihood of 5,000 other employees in the company."

The teamsters, convinced of the righteousness of their cause, go out on strike, but only against this one supermarket company in the area—the target company.

By noontime of the first day of the strike, the management of the company is beginning to have some second thoughts. Their competitors' trucks are still rolling, their competitors' stores are being supplied with fresh merchandise, and some of the struck company's customers are finding it necessary or convenient to go to another company's supermarket. If the strike goes on very long, some of those customers may not come back.

The company management may end by thinking, What are we going to gain by resisting? We'll lose sales, our competitors will gain, and when it is over we'll all be paying the same teamsters' wage scale anyway. Whatever we settle for will become the pattern for the industry; so how can we win? Also, if we give in to the teamsters it doesn't necessarily mean that the pattern will spread to our other employees, or at least not right away. If it does spread in the long run to the other employees, the same will be true for our competitors.

The president is likely to conclude, "As far as I can

see, if I let this strike continue all I'm going to do is lose business, and that will not help either the stockholders or the rest of the employees. If I give in, our competitors will face the same condition we do, so our profitability shouldn't be affected adversely. Also, the teamster payroll only amounts to 5 percent of the total, and this should help to ease the adjustment problem."

That night the company capitulates. To carry the story still further, not only does this settlement become a pattern for the area, but teamsters all over the country decide that what is right for one area is right for them too, and the pattern spreads through the land. And not only for the teamsters! The steelworkers, the auto workers, and others join in the parade while employers, by a reasoning process similar to that outlined above, capitulate in one area after another. In time, the settlements with the unions will also have a significant impact on unorganized workers' settlements and adjustments as well.

Thus the whole wage and salary edifice goes ratcheting upward, irrespective of the degree of pressure in the labor market as measured by unemployment. Profits and prices also go upward, as our statistics show. The workers start by trying to get for themselves a piece of the profits pie (after all it's big!), but as the profits go up along with wages and salaries the division of the pie as between profits and wages and salaries doesn't change appreciably. It's just that the price level goes up and up still further.

LABOR MARKET STRUCTURE THE REAL CAUSE

The above example is of course an extreme one, and probably no real-life situation matches it in exact detail.

Yet I submit that it contains the essence of the way in which the collective bargaining situation contributes to an inflationary wage-price spiral. Note that this essence consists of conditions in particular markets that relate to the structure of bargaining, and not to union power as such. The employer plays a part, too.

The main ingredient necessary for the upratcheting process is the organization on a market-wide basis of at least the employees, and perhaps also (but not necessarily) the employers, resulting in a market-wide pattern. It is this which makes it senseless for the employer to resist union demands. As long as any pattern agreed to by one employer will spread to his competitors (and of course there are some limits beyond which this will not occur) he has every incentive to give in.

This can be contrasted with the nonunion situation (our bookkeeper) where the employer will think twice about granting any outsized increase to his employees, for in his case there is no guarantee that the settlement will become a pattern for the market as a whole, and even if it should he may have more incentive to resist a "too large" increase. Particularly if there is any slack in the market, the individual employer, no matter how large, has every incentive to keep his voluntary wage adjustments within bounds. But where the market is organized by a union he has every incentive to give in.

This tendency for employers to give in too easily to union demands even caught the attention of Adolph A. Berle, one of the early New Dealers, famous for his book written with Gardner C. Means, *The Modern Corporation and Private Property.* In a speech in 1956, Berle commented on the regular annual wage increase which was then coming into fashion:

Our ancestors feared that corporations had no conscience. We are treated to the colder, more modern fear that perhaps they do.[24]

Although we may castigate the employer for not resisting the union sternly enough, his lack of resistance does not grow out of moral weakness but out of the structural situation which makes it bad business for him to resist. And note that the rate of unemployment, either generally or in the particular craft, has very little to do with the outcome once the union has decided to press its demands. This is because, unlike the situation in nonunionized markets, the employer does not have the option (nor, we assume, do his competitors) of hiring the unemployed at less than contract rates. The rates the employer pays are determined by the contract and by nothing else.

Now if unemployment is high in a particular trade it may induce the union to avoid large increases that may further reduce employment. But then again it may not. For if the union decides to press for large settlements and let the rate of employment go hang, as perhaps has happened over the years in coal and parts of the building industry, then it would appear that the union has the power to do so, in the sense that employers have very weak incentives to resist so long as they believe that a settlement for one is a settlement for all. It follows that there is no good basis for determining just how far above an existing pattern a union's demands may go. There really is little pressure to hold down settlements, such as comes from the market in the nonunionized situation.

Notice also, in the unionized situation, that the size of the employer doesn't make much difference. It is the effect of a capitulation on one's competitors that is important. For example, it might make more sense for General

Motors to resist an outsize settlement with the United Auto Workers than for a small housebuilder to resist a very large settlement with the plasterers. If General Motors goes on the assumption that anything it agrees to will likely become the pattern for the industry, with only minor variations to fit particular local conditions, it will not need to be greatly concerned about the effect of a settlement on its competitive position *vis a vis* its domestic competitors. But it *will* have to consider the effect of its actions on the competitiveness of the domestic auto industry as against imports of automobiles, and also as against other goods and services that compete for the consumer's dollar. These latter might include trips by air and other public transportation, household durables, and ultimately the whole range of expenditures open to consumers.

Of course, to the extent that General Motors feels that any settlement it makes will spread not only to its domestic automobile competitors but to the producers of other goods and services as well, its willingness to resist union demands will be weakened. But obviously there will be limits to this, particularly so far as its foreign competitors are concerned, and hence it will be anxious not to get too far ahead of the parade of wage changes.

Contrast this with the situation of a small housebuilder in a market like Chicago. Let us assume he has a 100-home subdivision under way, with ten homes already under construction. The plasterers go out on strike, demanding a 20 percent wage increase. What incentive does the contractor have to resist? Very little, actually. It will take a very large contractor to worry that any outsize settlement to the plasterers in Chicago will infringe greatly on his competitive position, at least against other contractors in Chicago; and of course he doesn't have to worry that some contractor from Denver, for example, may cut in on the market enjoyed by Chicago plasterers. Perhaps a really large contractor might worry that any increase granted to the plasterers might set a pattern for the other building trades in the area and raise the cost of buildings in Chicago to the point where potential buyers of houses would be encouraged to buy mobile homes instead. Even here, however, the builder might feel that he is protected by the zoning ordinances that govern the kinds of houses that can be built in his market.

Our small builder will hardly give this a thought, however. He has ten houses under construction, and the plasterers make up only a small part of his total costs. He may even have a pass-through escalator clause in his contracts that allows him to add higher labor costs to the price of his houses, and in future contracts he need not worry because his competitors will face the same increase.

This is why the construction industry witnessed some of the largest wage increases of any industry until restrained directly by the Construction Industry Stabilization Committee, despite the fact that unemployment in the construction industry tends to run well above the average of industry generally.

Once again we see that in the kind of market situation where bargaining takes place on a marketwide basis, even though the market is a small one and dominated by small companies, the rate of unemployment is not especially significant in determining whether or not there will be a wage increase or what its size will be. Apparently this has been true for a long time. From 1860 to 1869, according to S. Lebergott's figures, increases in the

Middle Atlantic states for carpenters amounted to 98 percent compared with 49 percent for common labor.[25]

BLAME THE SYSTEM—NOT THE UNIONS

Let us be clear that we are not opposing unions as such; nor are we trying to point the finger of blame at them as the chief architects of inflation because their demands for wage increases are beyond the amount that can be supplied from growth in output per person. Instead of castigating unions for seeking exorbitant wage increases, one could with equal logic lay the blame on employers for not putting up more resistance to these wage demands.

In this case the problem grows out of particular market situations in which the employer has little incentive to resist wage demands vigorously. This wouldn't be too much of a problem if such cases were limited in number and did not have significance for the *general* level of wages, as apparently they did not in the United States before the mid-1930s when the extent of unionism was small. If that were the situation, an outsize settlement in the construction industry, for example, would be like "a shot heard in the immediate vicinity," without significance for wage trends in general. The attitude might be, "If the construction unions want to price themselves out of the market, it's no skin off my back."

But today a settlement in the construction industry is not an isolated event, of no concern to others. The teamsters will take notice, to say nothing of the steel and auto workers. What one does will tend to set a pattern for others and, given marketwide organization and bargaining, employers will tend to give in to these spreading demands. Not only that, the union settlements tend to set a pattern which may later be followed for nonunion employees, though there may be some lags depending on the state of business conditions.

THE TAIL WAGS THE DOG

We seem to be looking at a situation in which the ordinary chain of cause and effect has been reversed. For example, the pattern-breaking settlement with the airline flight engineers in 1966 seems to have started a course of settlements which broke down the wage-price guideposts of the 1960s. One might blame that on the generally overfull employment situation of early 1966 (if 3.8 percent unemployment can be called overfull employment). But then, what about 1970? In the spring of 1970, the teamsters settlement started a chain of settlements in construction and then in autos and steel which were clearly unsupportable without price increases, despite the fact that the economy was then operating with a substantial margin of excess capacity and unemployment.

The inflation of 1973 was clearly of the old-fashioned demand-induced variety and, in fact, wage settlements in both the union and nonunion sectors were relatively restrained compared with what might have been expected in light of the large increases in the cost of living. However, 1973 and 1974 involve a number of special factors, so we will defer a consideration of this episode until Chapter 8.

Thus, leaving 1973–74 aside temporarily, the long-run inflation problem appears to stem from particular market situations in which wage adjustments are not responsive to the state of unemployment. This unresponsiveness exists for the simple reason that employers are not able to replace their workers with unemployed workers at less than going rates. In this sense there is a lack of competition in some labor markets that far exceeds any found in product markets, where buyers always have the alternative of a substitute.

Thus, given marketwide bargaining, wage settlements are not seriously hindered by the fact that demand may be down, as in the construction industry for example. If we accept that union settlements under our particular bargaining institutions are to a considerable degree independent of economic conditions in general, or in the particular area where settlements are taking place, and if we take one further step and say that union settlements in one area have a significant impact on other union settlements, and ultimately on the level of nonunion settlements, we have a situation in which wage and salary rates, and costs per unit of output, can move within wide limits independently of the general state of demand. It goes without saying that they will also move in response to changes in demand.

If we now take the additional step of saying that, in the long run at least, wage costs and prices will move in parallel, as proved by statistics extending over a long period of time, we must conclude that for the unionized sector prices will respond to changes in costs rather than to shifts in demand. This will be particularly true if the price elasticity of demand for such products is relatively low in the short run, i.e., if the quantity demanded is relatively insensitive to moderate changes in price, as would appear to be true for many durable goods (materials as well as finished goods). Then inflation can proceed at a rather arbitrary rate, depending fundamentally on the rate of increase in wage settlements in the unionized sector.

DO UNIONS AFFECT THE GENERAL LEVEL OF ALL WAGES?

The foregoing analysis rests on the assumption that one union settlement affects other union settlements and that these in turn influence nonunion settlements and the general level of wage and salary rates. Let us therefore review some of the evidence on the relationship between union and nonunion wages.

It is argued by some that unions do succeed in raising the wages of their members compared to what they would be if the employees were not organized and, by implication, compared to wages in unorganized areas. Common sense suggests that this is the case. Beyond the dictates of common sense, Professor H. Gregg Lewis of the University of Chicago has summarized a large body of research on the effect of unionization in many industries and has concluded that unions appear to have raised wages about 10 to 15 percent above the level of nonunion wages for comparable occupations.[26]

Assuming for the moment that Lewis's findings are correct, we need to raise another question: Do the higher wages for union employees come at the expense of profits, or are they made possible by lower wages for nonunion employees than would exist in the absence of unionization? If the former is the answer—that the higher union-negotiated wages are paid out of reduced profits—we would expect that the share of wages and salaries in total income or product would rise, and that the share going to property would fall. As we argued earlier, there is no good evidence that this is the case. In fact there is a remarkable stability in the share of product going to labor as against the share going to property, or, between the share going to capacity inside the skin as compared with that outside the skin.

This means that if unions raise wages above what they would otherwise be for these occupations, and if there is no evidence that the gain is at the expense of profits or, more generally, of property income, then the gain for the union members must be at the expense of wage and salary earners who are not in unions.

The way this might come about can be easily imagined. At the higher wages negotiated by unions, a smaller number of people will be employed in the unionized areas than would otherwise be the case. This will increase the number of people seeking employment in nonunion occupations and drive down their wages and salaries to induce employers in the nonunionized sector to hire the larger number.

This means, of course, that there will be a misallocation of resources. Too few people will be employed in the unionized area, since prices charged for products from this area must be high enough to cover normal profits plus above-average wages. And too many people will be employed in the nonunionized areas as evidenced by the fact that prices are high enough to cover normal profits (otherwise output would decline) plus wages which are below the average.

The general public would therefore gain if there were a transfer of employment from the nonunion to the unionized area of the economy, since they would be giving up a product with a below-average unit value for one with an above-average unit value (labor under these conditions would produce a higher value if employed in the unionized sector than if employed in the nonunioin sector). The transfer should continue to the point where the returns to both labor and capital would be equalized. It goes without saying that the nonunion employees would gain from such a transfer.

Now all of this is based on the assumption that unions do in fact raise the wages of union members above what they would be otherwise. As we said, both casual observation and numerous research studies suggest that this is the case. More recently, however, this conclusion has come into question. As that careful scholar, H. Gregg Lewis, himself observes:

. . . it appears to be true of studies of the relative wage impact of unionism that the estimates of the relative wage effects typically tend to diminish in size as they become more refined, especially as the factors other than unionism affecting wages are more completely controlled.[27]

L. W. Weiss, in a detailed study of finely drawn industry classifications, found that the higher earnings in concentrated than in non-concentrated industries are attributable largely to personal characteristics, or differing qualities of employees. As he concludes:

Once personal characteristics are introduced, the relationship between concentration and earnings is no longer significant and is negative about as often as it is positive. . . . The laborers in concentrated industries seem to receive no more for their services than they might in alternative employment for persons with similar personal characteristics. Their earnings contain little or no monopoly rent.[28]

Since the concentrated industries are highly unionized, while the non-concentrated industries are less organized, this implies that any hike in labor costs in the union sector will be communicated to the nonunion sector, possibly by a change in nominal wages but, at least in part, by a shift of "better-quality" people to the union area (which would offset in wage costs some of the rise in nominal wages) and a shift of "lower-quality" people to the nonunion area (which will raise costs even if nominal wages don't rise).

It should be noted that in the Weiss study one of the qualitative factors, or personal characteristics, is race. This comes close to being a rather circular form of reasoning: White people earn more than nonwhites because they are of "higher quality," but the main reason they appear to be of higher quality is that they earn more, that is, apart from differences in such things as education and training which are otherwise accounted for in the study.

Thus, while most observers, including Weiss, seem to agree that unions do in fact raise the wages of their members, it is not entirely clear whether this is at the expense of nonunion workers or whether the initial upratcheting of wages in the union sector is in time communicated through market forces to the nonunion area. At any specific time, probably both effects are present.

The effect of unionization on the distribution of income and of output is important because unions occupy a strategic place in the scenario of inflation as this writer sees it. It follows that if something is to be done about solving the inflation problem, we will have to change our present institutions affecting unions. Thus it is important that we reach a conclusion about the values unions contribute to the general welfare, that is, to you and to me.

DO UNIONS BENEFIT THE GENERAL PUBLIC?

Drawing airtight conclusions on the overall contribution of unions to the general welfare involves a wide area of uncertainty, try as we may to be objective about it. What we can say with some certainty is that from an economic point of view, apart from any relation unions may have to the inflation problem, they are at best neutral in their effect on the welfare of society while at the worst they may do positive harm. For example, to the extent that unions succeed in raising wages for union employees relative to wages of nonunion employees of otherwise comparable characteristics, there will be a misallocation of labor resources in the sense that society would benefit from an increase in the number of people working in the unionized industries and a reduction of the number in the nonunionized industries. The general public on average, and the nonunion group in particular, would gain from the tradeoff, though of course it is likely that the union group would lose.

But it is not entirely certain that unions do in fact raise wages for union employees relative to those of nonunion employees of *otherwise* comparable *characteristics*. If not, then it appears that the difference between union and nonunion wages is accounted for by quality differences between union and nonunion workers. As we noted previously, a major quality difference in Weiss's study of this subject is race. To the extent that union bargaining forces up union rates, and to the extent that this causes non-whites to gravitate away from the higher-paying occupations to the nonunionized lower-paying ones, the existence of unionism just adds one more discrimination to the many that confront nonwhite people in their efforts to raise their standard of life. It can hardly be condoned, or at least extolled, in a society that stands for equality of opportunity in the pursuit of happiness.

Thus from an economic standpoint, and from some social standpoints as well, it is hard to see that unions make any positive contribution to the general welfare. What they gain for their members is at the expense not of profiteering capitalists, as we saw earlier, but of their fellow workers unlucky enough to be outside of unions. And since we have argued that unions, or at least market-wide collective bargaining arrangements, are close to the heart of the cost-push aspects of the inflation problem, it would seem logical to argue that unions should be abolished. If unions were outlawed, employers would bargain with individual workers and would have strong incentives to hold pay increases within narrow bounds, just as our employer had with his bookkeeper at the beginning of this chapter.

But of course there there are other facets to the subject, mostly of a social nature which it is difficult for the economist to evaluate in any quantitative sense. For example, a union member may get great satisfaction out of "belonging" to a group and being proud of his craft, as a journeyman meat cutter, for example. He probably feels a certain security and derives an independence of spirit from being a union member, characteristics we like to see in a land professing freedom and the welfare of the individual. Also, it is likely that unions help to improve working conditions from the standpoint of the health and comfort of the worker.

Some economists might argue on the other side that a fully employed economy is the best guarantee of personal freedom and satisfaction to the worker. For if business declines very far, some persons will be unemployed, whether or not they are union members. In contrast, if the economy is at a level of full employment, a worker of merit with a widely used skill can thumb his nose at one employer and get as good a job across the street.

Let us grant that unions do bring a net social benefit —even though it is difficult to weigh the gains to union members against the probable harm to some parts of the public who may be excluded from unions for one reason or another. If we can find a way to suggest modifications in our existing institutions relating to unions, which will preserve their social benefits while doing away with their inflationary effects, we needn't worry about the tradeoff between social benefit and economic harm. The possible remedies are quite simple, and consist of two kinds: (1) introducing competition into the labor market, and (2) applying direct controls to labor settlements in the union-ized sector. We shall discuss these in turn.

SHOULD WE INCREASE COMPETITION IN THE LABOR MARKET?

As we consider what might be done to introduce competition into the labor market and why this might contribute to moderating or eliminating the inflation problem, we should keep in mind that the essence of the competitive system is that the individual is offered a choice. Sometimes we call it the *free* competitive system, by which we mean that the consumer, for example, is free to choose among suppliers of a given product or service, such as competing brands of cola drinks, or is free to choose among sellers of different kinds of products entirely—for example, Seven-Up vs. Coca Cola, Hershey bars or what have you. This is how the customer gets what he or she wants.

Let us review again in summary fashion how this works. A housewife in a supermarket surveys the many goods and services competing for her attention. She chooses among the various items available based on their relative contribution to the welfare of herself and her family, giving consideration to the relative prices at which they are offered and her evaluation of the contribution each will make to the family welfare. She may be influenced by advertising, "cents-off" coupons, or the location of the item on the shelf. But whatever the blandishments and influences other than price, she is the one who ultimately makes the decision as to the value of different items to her and her family.

Producers in turn will hire labor, rent buildings, and buy machinery in the hope of offering a product that will meet with the cutomer's favor in the sense that it can be sold at a price which will not only cover all costs in the usual sense of the term, including promotional and related items, but will also yield a profit at least comparable to what the average seller is able to earn on his property investment. If an individuial seller is not able to do this, he is evidently not supplying the customer with as good a value as she thinks she gets from something else. This seller will not be able to generate the funds for expansion, or possibly even for the maintenance of his business; others will be reluctant to advance him the necessary money; and as a result his output will decline.

On the other hand, if the seller is able to supply a product at a price which not only covers all his expenses but in turn yields a profit that is equal to or beyond the average rate of return on investment in the economy generally, this will give him the funds for expansion directly and will also make it easier for him to expand by securing funds from others. Also, the fact that profits are high in this endeavor will likely induce others to enter the business. This of course will increase production of the item and bring down its price, making it available to a wider range of buyers.

Thus so long as individuals and businesses are free to choose what they will buy and what they will make or do for a livelihood, the system will operate to maximize the production of goods and services the consumer wants. Anything that interferes with the freedom of choice of the consumer, or the freedom of individuals and businesses to expand their businesses or enter other businesses, will inhibit the ability of the system to perform this function. That is why we have laws against monopoly.

We should note at this point that even the greatest monopoly will not be able to deny free choice to consumers. There will always be some other product that can be substituted and will do the job either in part, or partly as well, though probably at higher cost, than the item being monopolized.

Let us take electricity as an example. Even if the price of electricity were not regulated, and a utility were allowed to charge what it wished, the availability of gas and oil would place some limit on the price that could be charged and hence some limit on the profits the utility could earn. This competition would be more effective in some uses than in others; in heating or cooking, for example, as against lighting in the home. The presence of a monopoly earning excessive profits would mean, of course, that the consumer would be receiving less of the more monopolized item (electricity) and more of the

nonmonopolized items (oil and gas) than would yield a
maximum of welfare in terms of the resources available.
This is because a given amount of resources would produce a larger value in dollars' worth of electricity than
in dollars' worth of oil and gas, so that consumers would
gain by having resources moved from the production of
oil and gas to the production of electricity.

Unfortunately, some things are to a greater or lesser
degree natural monopolies, such as electricity or certain
raw materials like aluminum. In addition, patents and
copyrights create legal monopolies of particular items.
This is done to encourage constructive innovation and
the development of new things. The granting of patents
and the creation of a monopoly in Xeroxing for example,
is presumed to be in the public interest because the creation of the Xerox process made copying more advanta-
geous than it was before with other products. Of course,
other products still compete with the Xerox, and in due
course the patents will run out so that anyone can use
the process. By that time, of course, it is possible that
Xerox Corporation will have pulled some other rabbit
out of its hat.

This brings out the fact that monopoly elements are
not necessarily all bad to the extent that they lead to
innovation and development beyond what might occur
otherwise. This perhaps is why in farming, for example,
where there are generally few monopoly elements, many
of the advances are made not by those involved in the
production of farm commodities but by the land grant
colleges and agricultural experiment stations subsidized
by the public purse. In other lines where monopoly elements prevail, as in photography and drugs, advances are
usually introduced by individual manufacturers.

With this refresher on the working of the competitive system, let us return to the labor market. The antitrust laws to the contrary notwithstanding, freedom in the labor market is just as essential to the efficient functioning of this market as it is in the market for products. In the case of the labor market, however, the businessman is in the position of the consumer, and the prospective worker is seeking to sell him his labor services.

Let us examine how this works. We will ignore land and capital equipment at this point in the interest of simplifying the argument. The businessman will be under the prod of avoiding losses and of trying to make as much profit as possible. He will hire labor to make products or to offer a service to consumers as long as he can do so profitably. Since others will be trying to do the same thing (assuming now that times are good and that people can generally find jobs with little difficulty), any employer will have to offer wages and salaries which, all things considered, including fringe benefits and working conditions, are as good as those anybody else will offer. Since the individual is free to seek the best job he can find (and since we are assuming that jobs are generally available), no employer will be able for very long to hold wages and salaries below a going rate. At the same time, however, given his constraint to earn a profit, or avoid losses, he also has every incentive to hold his wage and salary payments to the minimum consistent with maintaining and developing an efficient, enthusiastic workforce.

In this situation, where there is no union and he deals with individuals, an employer will be constrained by the profit-loss motive from paying more than the "going market" for the kind of people he wishes to have on his payroll; and the freedom of individuals to move will insure that he pays the going market rate so long as other opportunities are available—recognizing of course that a person will not wish to move in response to temporary conditions, and that people who are older and settled may not wish to change their occupations or locations, although their sons and daughters will, and maybe their friends.

In general, if we assume a situation of reasonably full employment, with a steady demand for the output of business, there is no reason to believe that wages and salaries, individual differences considered, wouldn't tend to continue at the same general level indefinitely, without change. It is like the example of our bookkeeper, generalized to the whole economy. Our bookkeeper will stay put as long as she thinks she is being treated fairly, is earning as much as she could elsewhere, or that there are other offsetting advantages such as hours, transportation, etc. This also assumes that she is getting a normal increase for her job, say 3 percent a year, plus some advancement in grade toward chief accountant. (We pick 3 percent a year for her particular job because this is roughly the long-run average of annual gain in productivity or output per man/hour generally.) This is what economists call an equilibrium situation.

We assume in this an equilibrium for the whole economy at something that might be accepted as "full employment," and we assume that general demand conditions are maintained at this point, with just enough stimulus from monetary and fiscal policy to produce a general growth in demand at a rate that will absorb the gradually rising ability to produce, i.e., an increase of about 3 percent a year per person employed. Now, practically, it would be difficult to fine-tune the economy so exactly that it would move steadily upward in a progression of just 3 percent a year per person employed, but there is no reason to expect that the economy itself would tend to develop either inflationary or deflationary tendencies from minor fluctuations about this target.

This book is not meant to be about the techniques for maintaining the economy on a steadily rising full employment track. The accepted techniques for doing this involve the appropriate use of monetary and fiscal policy (in that order, we would agree) and will not be elaborated upon here. It will be worthwhile, however, to spend a moment examining the way in which a too-expansive monetary-fiscal policy might create a general inflationary condition. If, for example, the government embarks on a new program of income support at a higher level for those on welfare, and no other changes are made in taxes or in interest rates, total incomes in the economy will rise above the track they were on previously. Human nature being what it is, and given the pressures working upon those on welfare, total spending in the economy will also rise above the track it was on previously. This means in turn that the total receipts of businesses and governmental entities will also rise, profits will increase, and businesses will try to expand. They will try to hire more people by offering higher wages and by paying higher wages to those now in their employ to keep them from being hired away by others. This will add further to money incomes, to spending, to receipts, etc., etc.

Round and round the economy will spiral upward, unless offsetting action is taken through a rise in taxes or a rise in interest rates, either or both of which will squeeze out certain demands previously being met so that those getting the increased welfare payments will be able to spend more. In the absence of such offsetting action, we will have what is known as a demand-induced or "demand pull" type of inflation. The total amount of spending by consumers, business, and government is just greater than the amount of product that the economy is capable of producing with its existing manpower and other resources. Consumers, businesses, and governments, in their efforts to bid the available products and resources away from each other, generate an incomes-price spiral, or what we loosely call a "wage-price" spiral. Such a wage-price spiral can be kept under control, at least conceptually, merely by keeping demand under proper control through an appropriate fiscal-monetary policy combination.

Now, however, let us introduce a union into the picture. This will enable us to see just what difference the union makes and what must be done in a union-management bargaining situation if the economy is to remain in a situation where control of total demand will be sufficient to keep the price level under control. The important thing to note here is that the power of the union as such is not the important thing. Rather, the important element is what goes on in the mind of the employer to affect his attitude toward settling with the union. This will depend a good deal on his assessment of the effect any settlement he may make will have on a settlement for the market as a whole.

To illustrate this with an example, let us consider the steel industry. Let us take one company and assume it is negotiating with a union. The union strikes over the issue of wage demands. It wants a settlement that the manage-

ment thinks is out of line in the sense that it represents
a larger increase than is being granted elsewhere and is,
in the opinion of management, larger than would be
needed to keep the company's employees from going
elsewhere or impairing the long-run ability of the company to attract and hold a competent work force.

Now, under these conditions, if the union represents
only the employees in that *company,* or more clearly still,
if it represents only a local *plant* within the company, the
company will think twice before it will give in to the
demands of the union. For it will consider that if it should
give in, this may have little effect on the pay scales of its
competitors in the steel industry, or of those in aluminum
or plastics, and therefore it will be saddled with higher
costs than its competitors. It might well figure that such
costs would be so excessive that in due course it would
be forced out of business. So it will resist the demand of
the union to the bitter end. Whether it is U.S. Steel or
some smaller producer, it will stick adamantly to its
stand. In time, the union will presumably come to see
the light and will modify its demands to something akin
to the "general pattern" of wage settlements.

On the other hand, let us assume that the union represents not only the workers in this particular plant but
steelworkers all over the United States, and that the union is picking on this company to set a pattern for the
industry. Immediately, the situation is quite different.
Even though the employer may think the union demand
is above the going pattern and is not necessary to keep
his work force intact, etc., as above, he has much less
incentive to resist than in the first case. This is because
giving in to the union will not necessarily impair his
competitive position. If he believes that the settlement

he makes will become a pattern for the industry—and perhaps for some of his competitors outside the industry, such as the aluminum industry—he will be much more willing to give in. And so, after a short strike when he finds he is losing business to his competitors, he will give in to the union.

Of course, if the strike is against all the producers in the industry rather than against just one, the incentive for management to capitulate may be somewhat less than if the strike is against only one. We say that it *may* be less because this will depend on the degree to which management believes the settlement will be generalized. Obviously, so long as only one is involved there may be some question about whether a settlement will be generalized to the industry. But if they are all in the same boat, there is little question that the settlement will be generalized to that industry, and probably there is some greater certainty that any pattern set in steel may become generalized to the whole economy. In any case, the incentive for the companies to resist is much less than if they were dealing individually with individual unions representing particular companies, or possibly only the individual plants within each company.

One can immediately see how a wage-price spiral can emerge from a bargaining situation in which, in effect, the union has a monopoly of the labor of a particular type in a particular market; or, in effect, establishes the price for such labor. Where we have collective bargaining on a marketwide scale—either for a national market such as steel, autos, or the services of airline pilots, or for a local market such as construction or haulage—and the employers have reason to believe that any settlement made will apply equally to all competitors, there is a powerful incentive for unions to ask for sizable settlements for their members and for employers to give in to these demands. Such settlements then tend to become generalized to other sectors of the economy through cumulative demands by unions in situations similar to that of the steel union, and given in to by employers in situations similar to that of the steel industry.

Bringing this down to the situation in our present-day economy, one can't help but feel that the gradual spread of the conviction that the economy will never again be allowed to fall far below the full employment level contributes to the confidence with which managements will be willing to assume that a wage pattern agreed to in one area may well spread elsewhere. Thus, not only will a particular company feel that it will not jeopardize its competitive position *vis á vis* its immediate competitors in its own industry by giving in to union demands, but that the pattern will spread to competitive products, materials or services before they can take advantage of any price differential. For example, a manufacturer's decision to shift from using steel to using aluminum, wood, or plastics because of a rise in the price of steel relative to these other materials, may involve a change in machinery, layout, etc., and would not be made lightly overnight. Also, the user of the material may need to be satisfied that the rise in the price of steel is permanent and not just a temporary phenomenon.

We are saying that where labor markets are organized competitively, i.e., where the employer may choose among actual and potential employees, the employer will be constrained by market forces to pay the going rate. Otherwise employees will go elsewhere. But, more important, the employer will also be constrained by market forces not to pay very much more than the going rate, for if he did it would raise his costs and lower his profits compared with those of his competitors. So long as the employer believes his actions will not be followed by his competitors, he dare not pay much above the going rate.

In contrast, if the employer is dealing not with single employees, but with a union organized across market lines, the situation is vastly different. If the union demands an increase in wage rates above the previously going rates, and strikes one employer to obtain its demands, that employer has very little incentive to resist the demand if he can be confident that the settlement he makes will also apply to other employers in the market. For he will then not be damaged competitively. In such a market structure, the resistance by employers to wage demands will be very much weaker than in the case where employers cannot be sure that any wage they agree to with individual employees will be matched by their competitors. It is essential to note that this lack of employer resistance is related to the structure of the market for wage bargaining, and only in a very minor way to the degree of unemployment in the particular industry or in the economy generally.

Therefore, in the absence of direct restraint on wage and/or other incomes, if a wage-price spiral is to be prevented in an economy that tends to approach full employment on a more or less continuous basis, it is essential that the bargaining structure for wages and salaries be such that any single employer will have considerable doubts about whether any labor settlement he makes will be generalized to his competitors. Otherwise he will give in too easily to union demands. This means, at the very least, that bargaining should be on nothing larger than a company-wide basis in any market, assuming the absence of direct restraint on settlements.

In addition, it must be clear that a union representing the employees in a particular company should not have a *monopoly* of potential employees of a particular type in that company. That is, the employer should have the option, the alternative, of hiring people who may be available. Then if employment were a little slack generally and if, for example, the teamsters in a particular company went out on strike for higher wages and benefits, that employer should have the alternative of seeking out nonunion persons who might be hired and trained to drive trucks if he thinks he could find them. This is what is meant by a free competitive market, a competitive labor market.

We should point out that it might not be essential that this particular employer be willing and able to hire substitutes for his journeyman truck drivers; it would be enough that he fear that his competitors might be willing and able to do this.

Under the circumstances outlined in the previous two paragraphs, no employer would be willing to settle for wages and benefits which were out of pattern with amounts that others in the community were paying. Unions would also be under substantial compulsion to avoid making such demands for fear their members would lose their jobs and not be able to find substitutes elsewhere. The economy would, in effect, be in the same situation as in our example of the bookkeeper market; a small amount of slack in the labor market would be sufficient to keep wages rates from ballooning upward. Only if there were a general excess of demand, i.e., only if demand exceeded supply at the existing level of wages and salaries, would there be a general tendency for incomes to rise excessively.

What we are suggesting is that the power of unions to make excessive economic settlements could be abolished by limiting the right of collective bargaining to entities no larger than one company or, say, 100 employees, whichever is larger. Hopefully, this would enable unions to preserve whatever social justification they have, such as protecting the individual worker from oppressive treatment by his employer (except, of course, at the vice presidential level), and helping to promote actions and causes that may not be feasible on an individual basis but are desirable from the standpoint of the general good—including a concern with working conditions, safety precautions, and possibly such things as pollution control. If unions cannot justify their existence on this basis, but must rely on their power to extort better-than-average wage, salary, and benefit settlements for their members, then we would question whether their continued existence is justified from the standpoint of the general welfare.

RECAPITULATION AND SUMMARY ON COMPETITION IN LABOR MARKETS

Let us pause at this point to see how we arrived at this conclusion. We said at the beginning that prices and the payment of compensation per unit of output are very closely related in the long run, though there may be temporary departures from this relationship, as in different phases of the business cycle. The reason for this is that, at one and the same time, compensation makes up the major element in both costs and incomes. Thus a general rise in wage costs will push up prices on the one hand, and on the other hand will supply the wherewithal by which the higher prices can be paid.

It goes without saying that real income—that is, the amount of goods and services available to be bought —depends purely and simply on our ability to produce. We cannot have something, as a nation, that is not produced. And the price of that production will be closely related to what is paid for it in wages, salaries, and benefits.

If prices, then, are to be kept stable in the long run, it is essential that total money compensation should increase no more rapidly than total production. To get it down to a per-person basis, this means that compensation per person on the average can rise no faster than production per person on the average, if prices are to be kept stable. And if output per person increases at the rate of 3 percent per year, and no faster, compensation per person on the average can rise no faster than 3 percent per year or else prices will rise.

We are saying also that where labor markets are structured competitively, where both the employer and the employee have a choice, as with our bookkeeper example, only a modest amount of slack in the labor market will suffice to keep particular wage and salary rates in consistent relationship to the general average of all wages and salaries. This general average in turn can be kept within the 3 percent boundary, or guidepost, by controlling the expansion of overall demand through appropriate monetary and fiscal policy. In that case a direct restraint on wages and salaries is not needed; monetary and fiscal policy can do the job alone.

Once marketwide unions enter the picture, however,

they will seek settlements above the 3 percent per annum norm for increases on the average. As Samuel Gompers is reputed to have said, unions always want "more." In this, of course, they are no different from anyone else. Who doesn't want just a little more than he already has, for his family if not for himself? The difference is that where unions have a monopoly of labor in a particular market they are in a position to get what they ask for, or at least something above 3 percent per annum, because employers have no strong incentive to resist their demands.

As a next step, we say that a pattern set by one group tends to spread to other groups in the community. This step rests on a somewhat more tenuous base than on the ability of unions to exact increases that are too large. But we can say that to the extent that a settlement in one area spreads to settlements in other areas, the whole compensation structure tends to rise. And if the rise is greater than can be offset by increased production per person, costs in general will rise and prices will too.

It is possible, we must admit, that if only a distinct minority of employees were organized across entire markets, whether the markets were large or small, this minority could extort higher wages and benefits for its members without raising the average for unorganized employees. This appears to have been the case for certain construction trades over a long period of time. However, since labor costs, on the average, are closely tied to prices, this means that if the construction workers pushed up their wages and others stayed the same, then wage costs would rise on the average. So would the average of prices for goods and services, assuming a rise in the cost of construction. Since nonunion wages are presumed not to have gone up, the gain by the construction workers would then only have been at the expense of the unorganized employees.

While such a development would still be possible, research has indicated that union wages on the average have generally not gained relative to nonunion wages for particular occupations in the postwar years, as we noted previously. This can only mean that in our postwar economy, given the present extent of unionism, and perhaps other factors such as the full employment expectation, an outsize settlement for one sector (some union) tends to become generalized to the whole economy. We say that the only way to stop this is to make the structure of the labor market truly competitive by prohibiting market-wide collective bargaining, or, alternatively, by direct controls. To fail to do one or the other, and perhaps initially both, is to guarantee that the inflation problem as we have known it will continue indefinitely.

This point—that the root of our postwar inflation problem lies in the structure of labor markets, that is, in our collective bargaining institutions—deserves emphasis because it is not widely understood or accepted. Until it is, there can be little hope of bringing inflation under control permanently. For only if it is understood by the general public will there be broad support for legislation to make the labor market competitive or to place direct controls on the operation of our collective bargaining institutions.

This is not to say that restraint in collective bargaining settlements is enough *alone* to keep down inflation. But we are saying it is a necessary if not sufficient condition. In addition, monetary-fiscal expansion must be restrained to keep overall demand from rising excessively. The experience of 1973–74 is clearly a case where excessive general demands combined with reduced food and energy supplies to produce a world wide inflationary explosion, as we will discuss more fully in Chapter 8.

WILL "TEMPORARY" CONTROLS DO THE JOB?

We will come back again to the need for a broad understanding of the problem as outlined above. But first let us deal with the wistful notion that somehow controls can be applied for a short time and then be allowed to slough off without inflationary consequences for the general price level. This is the standard line expounded by Nixon Administration economists who saw the root of the inflation of the latter 1960s as being grounded almost solely in the development of conditions of excess demand in the period following 1965. Their original prescription, as set forth in the February 1970 *Annual Report* of the Council of Economic Advisers, was therefore to stop the growth of demand and to open up a gap between actual and potential output. It was believed that opening up this gap would require only a minimal increase in unemployment:

. . . some increase in the rate of unemployment is possible.[29]
. . . small and temporary.[30]

But despite the fact that the actual increase in unemployment went well beyond the contemplated "small and temporary," thanks in part to the General Motors strike in late 1970, the price-wage spiral persisted. This caused the Administration economists some perplexity. As they said in the 1972 *Annual Report:*

Why the slowdown in the inflation was so halting and uncertain is another question which has not been clearly answered.

Although this phenomenon is often ascribed to "structural" changes in the economy, these structural changes are not unmistakenly evident. And although the delay in the disinflationary process was undoubtedly connected with the strength and duration of the inflation in the preceeding years, one could not be sure that this explanation alone was sufficient.[31]

Despite this bow to structural changes—to which we would ascribe the major share of the blame for the kind of inflation we suffered in the postwar years, again with the exception of 1973–74—the Administration apparently opted for the explanation that the failure of the original "game plan" to stem inflation resulted from expectations built up in previous years: the expectation of continuing inflation. For it used as its rationale for the direct controls introduced with the August 1971 freeze the idea that they would contribute toward eliminating this expectation of continuing inflation. As set forth in straightforward fashion in the January 1972 *Economic Report:*

The basic premise of the wage-price control system is that the inflation of 1970 and 1971 was the result of *expectations,* contracts, and patterns of behavior built up during the earlier period, beginning in 1965, when there was an inflationary excess of demand. Since there is no longer an excess of demand, the rate of inflation will subside *permanently* when this residue of the previous excess is removed. The *purpose of the control system* is to give the country a period of enforced stability in which expectations, contracts and behavior will become adapted to the fact that rapid inflation is no longer the prospective condition of American life. When that happens controls can be eliminated. (Italics added.)[32]

This implies that the economy, once the inflation is brought down to lower levels by controls, will not revert to inflationary tendencies in the absence of an inflationary excess demand. Of course we did not find out whether this would have been the outcome because the removal of controls in January 1973 was in fact accompanied by a burst of inflationary excess demand and an explosion of prices. Again we will leave further discussion of this episode to Chapter 8.

We have argued that prices and wage costs are closely tied together. Therefore, if wage and salary incomes are not held down to the point where labor costs per unit cease to rise rapidly, prices in the long run will rise to reflect the rising wage and salary costs. If price controls are used to hold nominal prices and price indexes below what they would be in a free market, the function of the price system in allocating resources will be thwarted and we will be back in a situation of shortages, probably of the items most desired by consumers, as became evident in Phase II and again in Phase IV of the controls introduced in August 1971. Such price controls always end by being dismantled.

COMPETITIVE LABOR MARKETS WOULD BE ONE ANSWER

Thus any system designed to produce reasonable stability of the price level must above all bring stability to the growth of incomes. One way is to introduce competition into the labor market by restricting the right of labor unions to bargain collectively. As we have argued, where employees are organized in a union across market lines, and the employer does not have the alternative of hiring other employees, the level of wages can be independent of market pressures to a high degree, and to a large extent irrespective of the rate of unemployment, because individual employers lack the incentive to resist union demands. But if the right of labor unions to bargain collectively should be limited to the company or plant level, and employers would have the alternative of hiring nonunion employees, the labor market would then be sufficiently responsive to changes in demand pressures brought about by monetary and fiscal policies so that we could have a stable price level with minimum levels of unemployment.

Three percent unemployment as the target for "full" employment does not seem at all unreasonable or incompatible with stable prices if collective bargaining could be limited to the company or plant level, and if employers would have the right to hire either union or nonunion labor. Because this would involve no interference with the working of the price system—in fact, it would free up some prices now arbitrarily set—it is the course to be preferred if we wish to promote a maximum of efficiency of the economic system.

However, it must be admitted at this point that we are engaging in wishful thinking if we assume that it will be easy for the public in general, and the labor unions in particular (to say nothing of the politicians), to agree to a substantial curtailment of the rights of unions. In our society, the general public must be convinced of the wisdom and desirability of an action before one can expect the politicians to take it up; or at least the politicians must be able to see that this is an issue on which they can make political capital and get themselves elected or reelected. And of course we wouldn't want it any other way, since we believe in representative government.

The public, however, is in general suspicious of business at this point in time, especially "Big Business." And

it has a lingering sympathy for the union as the representative of the little fellow, the underdog. One senses an
image in the public mind of a great bag of gold labelled
"profits" being carried up a steep hill on the backs of
countless straining and groaning working people.

Of course there is an element of truth in this. There
are people with above average incomes, and a few who
make it really big. But profits, as we have seen earlier,
are not that large. More important than the size of profits
relative to wages and salaries, however, is the fact that
within the confines of our free market system there is just
no simple way to alter quickly the tight relationship between them that has existed over a long period of years.
Hence, attempts to alter the distribution of income between wages and profits by raising wages merely end in
higher wage costs and hence in higher prices.

We hasten to point out, however, that it is still possible
to alter the distribution of income between wages and
profits as decreed by the market system. Profits can be
taxed as such, and are. Taxes on corporate profits in 1973
were $49.8 billion, according to the U.S. Department
of Commerce, or 40.6 percent of $122.7 billion of profits
before taxes. Taxes on personal income (including $29.6
billion of dividends paid out of profits already taxed
once) came to $151.3 billion, or 14.3 percent of personal
income amounting to $1,055.0 billion. In addition,
$119.2 billion of sales and excise taxes were taken out
before calculating profits or personal income, but of
course paid for by individuals in the final analysis, as are
all taxes.[33]

There is no reason in theory why the split between
profits and wages/salaries can't be altered to the extent
desired through the tax route. Moreover, this should

have only minimal effects on the price level, and such effects as there might be would be one-shot influences and would not persist or tend to cumulate. Of course, too heavy a hand laid on profits might impair the incentives to efficiency and progress, as we saw with the nearly confiscatory levies on "excess" profits in World War II.

Thus there is nothing in the system of free markets as such that is incompatible with whatever notions the community may have as to equity in the distribution of income. We have every reason to expect that, if we altered our collective bargaining institutions to bring them into conformity with the precepts of free competitive markets, this would make possible the achievement of full employment through our tested tools of monetary and fiscal policy without creating inflationary pressures. This would be in the interest of the public in general, including wage and salary earners as a group, since the economy could be allowed to operate at a lower average rate of unemployment than has been possible with the stop-go policies of recent years.

One would think that such a sensible solution to our problem of unemployment with inflation would be heartily approved by the voting public and that they would demand it from their representatives in the Congress and from the President. But neither here nor anywhere else in the world does this approach seem to command wide support outside the halls of academe, and perhaps not even there. As we have noted, this lack of support seems to stem from a general antipathy to profits as such and a desire to help the common man raise his status.

It is an irony of practical existence that the desire of the public for equity or equality, and the desire to raise the level of living for the common man, should result in institutions which have the effect of lowering the average attainable standard of living. Our standard of living is lowered because our institutional setup requires us to operate under stop and go policies which make the level of employment, and hence of output, lower than they could be otherwise. Also, the price level for that lower real income is higher and less stable than would be desirable. As Frank Knight once said, "It isn't what people don't know that does the damage; it's what they know that ain't so!"[34]

The problem of unemployment along with inflation is not limited to the United States but is worldwide in scope. The British in particular have wrestled with the problem, trying approaches that appear to satisfy no one for long. They have come up with terms such as *stop-go* and *stagflation,* which describe the frustrations of the situation about as well as anything. Nowhere in the world has anyone really tried to use the free market system to attack the problem by introducing competition into the labor market. Probably the reason is the same as in the United States, i.e., the desire for equality, a general feeling that labor unions are on the side of the common man, and a widespread aversion to profits as such.

On the other hand, there has been a willingness world-wide to try direct controls on the economy from time to time, in ways which involve restraints on incomes in general and on wages and wage settlements in particular. We now turn to a discussion of experience with such efforts in the hope that they may offer part of the way out of the problem of persistent inflation.

5

Direct Controls: The American Guideposts of the 1960s

WHILE the public worldwide has not demanded a free market approach to solving the inflation problem, it has nevertheless been very sensitive to its persistence. Granted that the public still seems more concerned with maintaining full employment than with holding down the price level. That seems to be true both for the United States and for other countries. But inflation is a growing irritant. The public's concern for the problem has made it willing to attempt various forms of control over prices and incomes from time to time in the effort to halt inflation. While voters everywhere have ultimately lost patience with these controls in every instance, the controls have been imposed over long enough periods to suggest that they offer a possible approach to inflation control. Such an approach might allow us to achieve a reasonable stability of the price level without destroying our institutions related to collective bargaining.

110

It is therefore worthwhile to examine briefly the history of various nations with controls, looking at the different approaches that have been taken and the reasons why they have broken down and been abandoned. This will form the basis for proposing a viable system that we might adopt on a more or less permanent basis. This system would supplement monetary and fiscal policy to prevent inflation while, at the same time, preserving the efficiency of the free market system.

PREREQUISITES FOR SUCCESS

At the outset we should recognize that there are certain prerequisites if a scheme of controls is to be effective, just as there are if the free market system is to be effective. Number one is that the controls must operate to hold back the growth of incomes relative to the growth of physical production of goods and services; for any excess of income growth over output growth will of course ultimately be reflected in prices, though it might be dammed up for a time. Secondly, and perhaps of equal importance for the long-run success of controls, it will be necessary that they be sufficiently flexible to accommodate changes in demand and supply relationships for particular goods and services, as well as longer-range shifts in relative demands for different goods and services, and technological developments affecting their production costs.

With that in mind, we may observe that attempts at controls have ranged all the way from informal "jawboning" at particular price and wage developments to an out-and-out freeze of wages and prices. We shall now review this experience, starting with the experience of the United States with guideposts in the early 1960s, proceeding then to the British experience, turning next to the efforts of other western nations to handle the problem, and finally returning to review the U.S. experience with the more formalized controls of the period after August 1971.

THE KENNEDY-JOHNSON GUIDEPOSTS

The wage-price guideposts established by the Kennedy Administration in 1962 were an attempt to set standards for judging whether particular wage and price developments were in the public interest. They were couched in very cautious language—properly so, since when they were first promulgated in 1962 the country had witnessed a decade in which the consumer price index had risen by less than 2 percent a year on the average, and the wholesale price index by less than 1 percent per annum. At the same time, it was recognized that there were segments of the economy in which prices and wages might rise even though demand and supply conditions did not warrant it, although demand pressures could also be anticipated since it was the aim of the Kennedy economic policies to raise the level of demand in order to lower the rate of unemployment (which at the end of 1961 stood at 5.8 percent of the labor force).

The rationale for the guideposts was set forth clearly and concisely in the *Economic Report* of January 1962:

Wages and salaries are at the same time the principal cost to employers, the main source of income to employees, and the major source of demand to the economy as a whole.
If living standards are to rise over time, real wages must increase. Stability in the general price level means, therefore,

that average money wage rates should follow a generally rising path. As output per man-hour increases, rising money
wage rates can be absorbed into stable labor costs per unit of
output. So long as unit labor costs do not increase, rising
wages are fully compatible with stability in the price level.
Whatever its cause, a rising price level is characteristically
accompanied by a rate of wage increase in excess of the rate
of increase in output per man-hour.[35]

No one could summarize better the message that we
have been presenting in the course of our discussion up
to now. The *Report* then goes on in its cautious way to
state that when compensation rates per man-hour rise
more rapidly than output per man-hour ". . . prices
sooner or later will increase," but that if excess demand
pulls up prices then competition for labor will pull up
compensation per man-hour faster than output per man-
hour. As we have pointed out, prices and wage costs per
unit of output (i.e., compensation per man-hour divided
by output per man-hour) tend, like love and marriage,
to go together. That fact alone, however, does not estab-
lish which is the cause of the other.

While it is true that an excess demand inflation will be
accompanied by a rise in both prices and wage costs,
though not necessarily in the same percentage magnitude
in the short run, it is absolutely essential that wage costs
per unit be stabilized if the price level is likewise to be
stabilized.

In the long run, if we think of employment costs as
being arbitrarily determined, or "administered," to use
the economists' jargon, prices will follow employment
costs up, sideways, or down as well. In a perfectly competitive economy, or an economy in which competition
exists in the labor markets, irrespective of whether it

exists in the product markets, the regulation of demand alone will be sufficient to maintain a desired rate of increase of wage and salary rates, but to the extent that wages are administered they may change apart from any stimulus from demand conditions. The *Report* comes close to seeing this in the following passage:

Competitive behavior throughout the economy involves more than rivalry among firms selling similar products in a single market; it also involves hard bargaining between firms buying and selling from each other and between firms and unions. Abridgement of competition may be evidenced as much in permissive wage increases which are simply passed along in higher prices as in agreements among firms to divide markets.[36]

This may refer to "abridgement of competition" among employers rather than in labor markets, in which case it is wrong. As we noted earlier, rivalry among many employers in a single market is more likely to result in "permissive wage increases which are simply passed along in higher prices" than is a monopolisitic or oligopolistic structure among employers in a particular market, assuming marketwide organization of employees. We mentioned the construction trades as a particular example of this. Nevertheless, the above passage carries an interesting implication that it is the duty of management to be tough and to resist the demands of the unions, and this in the public interest! We would agree, to be sure, but it is not often that one sees in a political document (if the President's *Economic Report* can properly be called that) an admonition to businessmen to resist the demands of unions, assuming that is what is meant by "hard bargaining" on the part of a firm, and assuming further that we can equate behavior in the public interest with competitive behavior.

We may recognize that *as far as the price level is concerned* the question of monopoly is really only of major concern on the labor side of the market, though monopoly elements on the firm side of the market are undesirable for other reasons. But a political document must be even-handed: a statement about appropriate behavior for unions must be balanced by an equivalent admonition to employers. This is not to say that the economists who wrote the *Report* were insincere; more than likely they believed what they wrote. Even so, we can recognize that part of it, on analysis, just ain't so.

The evenhandedness is evident in the introductory remarks prefacing the presentation of the guideposts:

There are important segments of the economy where firms are large or employees well-organized, or both. In these sectors, private parties may exercise considerable discretion over the terms of wage bargains and price decisions. Thus, at least in the short run, there is considerable room for the exercise of private power and a parallel need for the assumption of private responsibility.[37]

And now for the guideposts by which to measure whether wage and price actions in particular cases are appropriate:

The general guide for noninflationary wage behavior is that the rate of increase in wage rates (including fringe benefits) in each industry be equal to the trend rate of over-all productivity increase. General acceptance of this guide would maintain stability of labor cost per unit of output for the economy as a whole—though not of course for individual industries.
The general guide for noninflationary price behavior calls for price reduction if the industry's rate of productivity increase exceeds the over-all rate—for this would mean declining unit labor costs; it calls for an appropriate increase in price if the opposite relationship prevails; and it calls for stable prices if the two rates of productivity increase are equal.[38]

These guideposts were subject to many qualifications and exceptions in the 1962 *Report.* They were repeated in subsequent *Reports,* but with less attention to the qualifications and exceptions. The 1964 *Report* carried a table which showed the rate of trend productivity for the private economy as 3.2 percent[39] and the 1966 *Report* called specific attention to this figure and recommended that the 3.2 percent be continued even though productivity in the most recent five years (the original basis for calculating the trend rate of productivity change) was 3.6 percent.[40]

In the 1966 *Report,* too, the Council took note that with the economy approaching full employment (it noted that unemployment was 4.1 percent of the labor force) the danger of price increases would become greater. But it took a generally optimistic view of the prospect for containing inflation, citing the apparent absence of a tendency for industrial prices to rise as they had in the 1950s and observing that: "The outlook for unit labor costs is good."[41] This was perhaps too sanguine a statement, for it wasn't too long afterward that a most unlikely group—not the autoworkers, nor the steelworkers, but the airline mechanics—succeeded in blowing the lid off the wage guidepost.

The 1966 airline settlement with the mechanics is of special interest because it illustrates the tendency for wage increases to become excessive first not so much in the oligopolisitic industries (autos and steel, for example), which presumably have great "market power," but in an industry in which the employers do not fear outside competition (the airlines, a regulated industry), in which the craft on strike represents only a small part of the total wage bill (the mechanics—somewhat like the teamsters in our supermarket example earlier), and in which the union has a monopoly of the particular trade. In fairness it should be noted that by 1966 wage increases in nonunion areas had begun to exceed the guideposts, although it is not entirely clear that this was true before the settlement with the airline mechanics.

In the January 1967 *Report* the Council continued to repeat the guidepost notion that compensation increases could not exceed the productivity gain if inflation was to be contained, but rather wistfully concluded that adherence to the guideposts was not likely in view of the large price increase (about 3½ percent for the Consumer Price Index) in the previous year. For all practical purposes the guideposts were dead from that point on, which merely goes to show that controls just won't work once exceptions start to be made, as with the airline mechanics. Whether it is practicable to try to enforce controls when demand pressures pass a certain point is another question, but we won't try to answer that at this point!

It seems reasonable to conclude that the guideposts were effective in holding down the growth of wages and prices in the period 1962–65, although after mid-1965 both prices and wages began to rise more rapidly. As John Sheahan summed it up in his 1967 study, *The Wage-Price Guideposts,* for the Brookings Institution:

The first four years of the guideposts' existence were characterized by a change toward greater stability of prices and wages. As compared to the immediately preceding four years of slower growth and higher unemployment, the rate of increase in prices was closely similar and the rate of increase in wages was less. As compared either to the whole postwar period from 1947 to 1961, or to 1953–61, both prices and wages were more nearly stable.
It is impossible to prove or to disprove the hypothesis that the

guideposts were an important factor in this achievement. This is because no one can be completely sure of what would have happened if they had not existed. Comparison to past relationships indicated simply that the period in which they were applied was one of considerable gain.

From mid-1965, both prices and wages began to rise more rapidly. This does not prove that the guideposts ceased to have any relevance. Neither prices nor wages went up as much as might have been expected in terms of earlier relationships.[42]

In other words, during the period of the guideposts, it appears that the Phillips curve shifted downward and to the left compared with the relationships existing in prior periods. That is, for any given level of unemployment, the percentage change in prices and wages was less than would have been expected on the basis of prior relationships. Other investigators, using a variety of statistical approaches, have reached similar conclusions.[43]

Since we know that in the more recent period the Phillips curve has shifted to the right and upward, we are apt to take the experience under the guideposts as offering fairly conclusive proof that they alone explain the favorable results in the period 1961–65. But it is possible that the period from the end of the Korean War to the early 1960s created a stability of expectations that would have made for more restraint in wages and prices even without the guideposts. As Lipsey has argued for the United Kingdom, and as we have observed earlier in connection with the U.S. data, it appears that the Phillips curve can shift about from time to time and that there is considerable question about whether there really is any long-run fixed relationship between wages and prices on the one hand and unemployment on the other.[44] At any rate, the period from the end of the Korean War to the

Guideposts witnessed three business recessions in the space of 7 years.

The facts alone do not resolve the uncertainty of whether prices and wages would have reacted as they did with or without the guideposts. However, it is of interest that by mid-1965, when the rise in both prices and wages began to accelerate, the unemployment rate was approaching 4.5 percent, a figure that it held in both July and August before proceeding lower. It is perhaps more than coincidental that the inflection point on the Eckstein-Brinner long-run Phillips curve is at 4½ percent unemployment—i.e., at this level of unemployment or below, the rate of price and wage rise shoots skyward. But based on experience during the period of the guideposts, from 1961 to 1965 as a whole, a 4½ percent rate of unemployment would be associated with only a 1 percent annual rise in industrial wholesale prices, according to a study by the Federal Reserve Bank of Cleveland alluded to by Sheahan.[45]

6

Direct Controls: The European Experience

WE TURN now to survey briefly the experience of the nations of Western Europe with price and wage controls of the relatively informal variety that goes by the name of "incomes policy." There are several things to keep in mind. First, many of the European efforts at incomes policy restraints grew out of economic devastation left by World War II. In this condition there was considerable agreement on both sides of the wage-price bargaining question that if there ever was a time to bury the class war hatchet, this was it. There was a great feeling of solidarity, of everyone being in the same boat, and therefore a willingness to tolerate controls and restraints in the interest of getting the economy back on its feet. As time went on this feeling of solidarity tended to fade away.

Second, as in the United States, we find that the debate over wages and prices tended to become a discussion about the division of the product between wages and profits. The myth apparently persists worldwide that somewhere there is a pot of gold called profits which can be tapped without limit to finance wage increases. Of course, every attempt to do so by raising wages in the market winds up not in an increased share of the product for wage and salary earners, but in a rise in the price level. The myth apparently dies hard. It should be noted that the European countries show the same relatively unchanging relationship between wages, gross profits, and prices over the years as the United States, though the statistics are by no means as clear as in the United States.

Third, there is a distinct difference between the European and American economies in terms of the average level of unemployment at which they operate. Unemployment in the European economies has been substantially less than in the United States without exception. This has contributed to a situation in which actual wage rate increases will usually exceed the rates and changes in rates provided for in contracts. This phenomenon is known as "wage drift"—the amount by which the increase in wages exceeds the amount contracted for. To some extent this wage drift reflects long-standing institutional practice in collective bargaining, but it also reflects excess demand pressure in the labor market which makes it worthwhile for employers to offer more than contract rates to keep their labor force or to attract additional workers.

It is of course rather difficult to maintain any direct controls in such a situation of extremely tight labor markets. In particular, in the key matter of holding down increases in wage and salary incomes, it becomes ex-

122

tremely difficult to keep the cooperation of labor union representatives for long. Even if those at the top might be disposed to go along with a wage stop or restraint, those down the line are apt to feel that they are entitled to take advantage of a situation which will allow them to obtain a larger wage increase than the guideline allows, and that if they don't someone else will. The feeling is that if a local labor leader wants to keep his job, he'd better anticipate such situations before a potential rival unseats him.

All of which is to say that while there are many similarities between the situations of the European economies and that of the United States, which makes it worthwhile to study their experience, there are also some differences, which means that their experience cannot be transferred to U.S. conditions without important modification in many cases.

THE UNITED KINGDOM*

With this background, let us launch our survey with Great Britain, which is closest to us in language and geography.

The Bargaining Climate

The United Kingdom stands about in the middle of European countries in the extent to which its labor force

---

* The factual material regarding The United Kingdom and the other countries covered in this chapter is drawn in large part from Lloyd Ulman and Robert J. Flanagan, *Wage Restraint: A Study of Incomes Policies in Western Europe,* University of California Press, Berkeley, 1971, and from J. Murray Edelman and R. W. Fleming, *The Politics of Wage-Price Decisions,* University of Illinois Press, Urbana, 1965.

is organized in unions. Unions control somewhat less than half of all employees registered in the national insurance system. This is substantially less than in Scandinavian countries but is substantially higher than in the United States, West Germany, France, or Italy.[46] There is an overall union association, the Trades Union Congress, but it has little direct control over the member unions, which are highly autonomous and organized largely along craft lines. The shop stewards in local units have substantial authority and often go their own way irrespective of what the national organization may be doing.

On the employer side there are two main associations: the Federation of British Industries which concerns itself primarily with technical and commercial matters, and the British Employers' Confederation whose Wages and Conditions Committee is the main instrument for overall bargaining. Like its counterpart on the labor side, however, the BEC exercises only moral suasion over its constituent associations, which often go in their own independent directions.

Chronology

Incomes policy in the United Kingdom started in 1948, with a Labor government in power and with a virtual freeze on wages and dividends. This was a voluntary program, but it is generally agreed that it exerted a moderating effect on wage changes into 1950. Prices were not covered. The consumer price index drifted upward moderately in 1949 and much of 1950. By the fall of 1950, however, prices were beginning to rise more rapidly and the program of wage restraint broke down.

The acceleration of price rises in 1950 apparently reflected world developments associated with the outbreak
of the Korean War. This shows that, given fixed exchange rates at least, it is difficult for an individual
country, even of the size of the United Kingdom, to
insulate itself from developments in outside markets.
When we get to looking at the incomes policy machinery
in Scandinavia we will see that it makes specific provision
for taking world developments into account.

The Conservatives were returned to power in 1951,
and thereupon cooperation from the TUC and the unions in wage restraint, always grudging at best, became
nonexistent. The government continued to urge wage
and price restraint, but this jawboning had little apparent
effect on the course of either wages or prices. In 1957
a Council on Prices, Productivity and Incomes was set
up which made several reports related to the inflation
problem. However, it blamed inflation on demand pull
almost exclusively. As we observed earlier, we have no
doubt that this was a major influence in Britain, but we
would expect that cost-push would also be a contributing
factor. In its final report, in 1961, the Council did place
a much greater emphasis on cost-push and advocated
some effort at income restraint.

In 1961 the U.K. was plagued by a balance of payments crisis. A pay pause for government workers was
announed in Commons. It was hoped that this would set
an example and that private and nongovernmental public
workers would follow suit. But the TUC, stating that the
government's decision had been reached without con-
sulting either the TUC or industry associations, refused
to go along.

In April 1962 the pay pause was supplanted by a guide-post approach similar to that set forth in that year for the U.S. In the U.K. it was called a "guiding light" at the specific level of 2 to 2½ percent, including wage drift, this representing the rate of productivity growth experienced in the U.K. There were some exceptions, of which at least two were significant: (1) a higher increase was permissible if there had been any special increase in productivity or (2) if it was "plainly necessary" to attract labor into an industry.

In an economy of relatively full employment, it is not hard to see that there might be many situations where it would be "plainly necessary" to pay higher wages to attract a work force. Also, it might not be too difficult to argue that there had been some special increase in productivity, or that some factor would lead to a significant improvement in productivity. Then, of course, once wages went up in the areas of necessity, other areas would need to be granted exceptions in a full employment economy or they would lose their workforce over a period of time. Be that as it may, wages actually went up by 4½ percent in 1962.

Parenthetically, we might mention that another board was set up in June 1962. This one was called the National Incomes Commission and consisted of five representatives from the public. There were no representatives from labor or management as such. The TUC refused to cooperate, saying this time that the government should work out the incomes policy directly with labor and management groups and should not try to pass the problem off to an "independent body." In any case the Commission's function was to examine pay settlements referred to it by the government and to report on them in the light of the guidelines. It had no direct authority to intervene and no authority to alter settlements submitted to it. Its function was largely educational, though it could make suggestions about future settlements. Its influence, however, was negligible and in 1963 the guideline was raised to 3½ percent. The rise in hourly earnings from 1963 to 1964 was 8.2 percent.

A more stringent form of incomes policy was introduced in 1964 following the election of a Labor government with which the TUC and the unions themselves were inclined to be more cooperative. The National Incomes Commission was replaced by the National Board for Prices and Incomes, on which both labor and management were represented. The guideline was reaffirmed at 3½ percent but with two new exceptions for added increases if existing wage scales were (1) too low for a decent standard of living or (2) out of line with similar work elsewhere. Also, this time a price guideline was included. There were to be no price increases at all, though there were exceptions in the event of cost increases (as with imported materials, for example). Also, the Board was to be given 30 days notice of intended changes in prices and wages. Further, the Board could and did intervene in particular disputes. Once again, however, the recommendations of the Board were purely advisory. There was no mechanism for enforcing its findings, and it was limited to recommendations.

As to the effectiveness of this newer form of incomes policy, suffice it to say that wages continued to rise at the rate of 8 to 10 percent per annum into the summer of 1966. Also, the exception for low-paid workers was another lever tending to push up the average of all wages. Much as one might sympathize with the objective of raising the pay of people who work at wages that afford less than a decent standard of living, there is no indication that attempting to do so by negotiating higher wage rates for low-paid groups (as distinguished, for example, from education and training designed to raise the worker's capability) will actually accomplish this objective, except possibly temporarily. Wage differentials tend to be restored in time. We shall see this particular aspect of incomes policy reappear, particularly in the Scandinavian countries where egalitarianism has been pursued even more vigorously, but we might say with like results.

The case is rather like that of minimum wage laws in the United States. However laudable the objective of raising the income of low-paid people, the main effect of legislating higher wages for the low-paid is to raise the pay of all workers because differentials tend to be restored. It may also tend to increase unemployment among those working at the lower levels. A more constructive approach to the same end would be to give these people more earning capacity through education and training, as of course will happen to a large portion of the young in any case.

By the summer of 1966 the continued rise of incomes, costs, and prices precipitated another balance of payments crisis in the United Kingdom. The government obtained the approval of both the TUC and the Federation of British Industries to a six-month standstill on wages, salaries, dividends, and prices. In fact, hourly earnings (and prices too) remained virtually stable for the six-month period. This was followed by six months of "severe restraint" and the extension of the zero guideline for prices to July 1968. Hourly earnings increased at a rate of only 1.9 percent in the first half of 1967, but

128

by April 1968 hourly earnings were up more than 8 percent from a year earlier. Nevertheless, the guideline was again set at 3½ percent for 1969 for wages, salaries, and dividends, but was raised to 4½ percent late in 1969. But by July 1970 the Labor government was out of power and this put an end to any further attempt at incomes policy, at least for the time being.

What did this experience prove? As two observers summed it up:

> If success is measured in terms of evidence that the government's campaign elicited acquiescence and/or support, failure is quite clear. Never, except for one brief period from 1948 to 1950, did the trade unions find it possible to agree, and even then a "wage pause" was put into effect without announcement. Our analysis further suggests that local managements have continued to put into effect wage increases despite national bargains which presumably settled the wage question, that national labor and management organizations are incapable of exerting other than moral influence over their members, and that in any event there is very great difficulty in defining and formulating an equitable wage policy.[47]

In light of this experience, the Conservative government that came into power in 1970 eschewed incomes policy and vowed it would never have anything to do with it. This is reminiscent of the Republicans' stance in the United States before August 1971. Nevertheless, as in the United States, incomes policy refused to die or even fade away because the problem to which it was addressed, however ineffectually, also refused to go away. Inflation and unemployment continued as twin problems (stagflation is the British word for it). And so it should perhaps come as no surprise that on July 19, 1971, the Federation of British Industries announced that its members had agreed to a 5 percent price increase ceiling and in general would try to avoid any increases except where they were "unavoidable," a necessary exception in a country where the cost of imports is beyond direct control.

The announcement by the Confederation was purely voluntary, and ostensibly was not inspired by the government which professed to have no faith in such policies. But at least the government did not oppose the action. It coincided with the adoption of a strong program to stimulate the economy, which of course added to the inflationary fuel. The stimulative actions included a cut in the purchase tax, the elimination of hire-purchase restrictions (like U.S. installment credit restrictions) and an increase in the allowance for the first-year writeoff of business equipment purchases from 60 percent to 80 percent. It was hoped that labor would follow the example of industry and suggest a program of restraint on its own; but, consistent with its posture previously when Conservative governments were in power, it refused to go along.

It will hardly come as a surprise that the march of inflation was slowed only briefly, that it resumed in the fall of 1971, and that it accelerated in 1972 to the point where by fall price increases were running at the rate of 10 percent and labor settlements at the rate of 17 percent per annum. The government was driven by late October to impose a 90-day freeze on prices and wages, which later was extended to the end of April 1973.

The freeze applied to all prices and charges for goods and services for domestic use. However, fresh foods were exempt; a direct pass-through was allowed for increased costs of raw materials and raw agricultural products, with fixed cash margins above costs. The wage freeze did not prevent increased pay for extra effort or output, as with piecework, nor for "genuine" promotions.

The freeze, known as Phase I, was followed by a more flexible Phase II covering the period from the end of April through November 1973. It provided for pay increases of one British pound per week plus 4 percent as a maximum, which amounted to approximately 8 percent of the average wage payment at the time. The Trades Union Congress said, however, that it would not support the guideline.

On prices, manufacturers were allowed to increase prices only where "unavoidable" cost incr.. .es had occurred, which put some pressure on businessmen to hold down wage and salary increases. Profit margins were strictly limited and could not exceed the best two of the last five years ended before April 30, 1973. Retailers, on the other hand, were allowed to apply their historical markup to costs, using whatever the markup percentage had been in the last complete year before the end of April 1973. However, net profits for retailers were limited in the same manner as for manufacturers.

Under Phase III, to cover the period from November 1973 to November 1974, prices were to be continued under tight control, although depreciation was to be allowed in calculating unit costs and there was some restriction on the extent to which profit margins could be reduced. Also, firms earning less than 8 percent on capital were freed from price control. As before, price controls did not apply to exports and fresh foods.

Pay increases in Phase III were to be limited to 7 percent, with a maximum equivalent to $840. However, extra amounts would be allowed for removing "anomalies and obstacles" and for better use of manpower. Also, cost-of-living adjustments would be allowed if the cost of living should rise by more than 7 percent above the level of October 1973.

Despite the regulations and controls, it was reported that the retail price index for October 1973 was up 2 percent from the month before and 9.9 percent from the year-ago month.

Evaluation

Perhaps nowhere else in the world have the frustrations confronting economic policymakers in the postwar years been more evident than in the United Kingdom, i.e., the problems of trying to attack both unemployment and inflation, sometimes simultaneously. The difficulties stem in part from the fact that the United Kingdom is very dependent on the outside world, with an international near-reserve currency for which it has only meager reserves, and therefore cannot stand for long an unfavorable balance of payments under the fixed exchange system. Yet it is not so dependent on the outside world that it is willing to gear its policies solely to adapting to changes originating elsewhere.

The result has been a policy of "stop-go," triggered largely by the status of its balance of payments, at least until the present period of floating exchange rates, and possibly contributing in no small measure to its overall record of inadequate growth in recent years. As E. H. Phelps Brown put it in 1966 in summarizing the steps that followed the development of a deficit in the balance of payments in an effort to stave off a run on the pound:

The countermeasures were traditional: higher interest rates, quantitative and qualitative restriction of credit, and a check on government spending together with higher taxes. These proved effective in meeting the crisis of the foreign exchanges. But at home they were associated with checks to investment and output and a rise in unemployment. A sharp political reaction expressed the disquiet of public opinion. Governments did not wait to see whether the continuance of monetary and fiscal restraints would prove compatible with a renewed rise of physical output but loosened the constraints as soon as they dared. Activity responded for two years or so; but then once more the balance of payments gave concern, and on went the brakes again. Periods of fairly rapid growth of industrial production—1953–55, 1959–60, and 1963–64—alternated with periods of little growth or none—1956–58, 1960–62, and 1965.[48]

While it cannot be said that the interjection of incomes policies into the stop-go process was a success, we cannot say that it was an outright failure either because we don't know what the situation really would have been if there had been no incomes policy at all. Nevertheless, it seems clear that the policies themselves were not adequate to hold inflation and the balance of payments in check and hence are not something that can be adopted without substantial modification as a viable long-run solution. The British experience does, however, point to a few conclusions that we may keep in mind as we move along.

1. The guidelines approach is aimed at a real problem, especially in the postwar British economy, of trying to keep the economy fully employed without inflation. Accomplishing this objective seems to be impossible through the now-traditional tools of monetary and fiscal policy alone, in the United Kingdom as in the United States.

2. The controls cannot work in an environment of too-full employment, where demand substantially exceeds capacity at existing price levels. This leads to a rise in wages (and presumably salaries as well) in areas not under the control of national union leadership, even though the latter may recognize the need for restraint. If the demand situation is such that local plant unions can push wages up above the norm, or if employers themselves bid them up above the norm, as happened frequently in Britain, it can hardly be expected that the union leadership at the national level can go on preaching moderation for long.

Demand conditions must be restrained sufficiently so that employers of their own volition do not go ahead raising the level of nonunion or union wages beyond the norm, and so that employers will strongly resist demands by local shop unions that go beyond the norm, without fearing that they will lose their labor force to another employer willing to pay more. On the basis of British experience, this suggests that the level of unemployment cannot be pressed much below 3 percent on U.S. definitions.

3. It is helpful if both labor and industry are represented on the body formulating and administering the incomes policy. The only times incomes policy seemed to be clearly effective were when they had the cooperation of at least the Trades Union Congress, if not labor as a whole.

4. The guidelines should have the force of law and there should be penalties for violating them. The purely advisory pronouncements of the Council on Prices, Productivity and Incomes, the National Incomes Commission, and the National Board for Prices and Incomes

appeared to have small effect in stemming the rising tide of wage and other income inflation, though of course we do not know what the situation might have been without them. But clearly they were not enough.

5. A guideline policy, to be successful, will need to have the understanding and backing of the public. This will require a much higher degree of sophistication in understanding the relationship between wages and other incomes, and between wages, costs, and prices, than appears to exist in ͟ne minds of the public at present. The lack of public understanding and support is evident in the government's attempt to buck the issue to independent nongovernmental bodies, and the general reluctance (often outright refusal) of the union leadership to go along with a policy of restraint. Neither politicians nor union leaders can get far out of step with their constituencies, and to a degree must cater to their prejudices. This suggests that professional educators have a unique responsibility to communicate with the public, but to a degree the cause must also be espoused by those who profess to be "leaders" in active life, whether this be in politics, unions, or business.

6. Exceptions to the application of a guideline must be held to a minimum; otherwise the exceptions create "inequities" themselves which can only be corrected by additional exceptions or which will be corrected anyway by action of the market itself. For example, one can sympathize with the desire to see people get more whose wages are substandard, or who may have made special efforts to adopt practices which improve productivity, and surely we don't want to discourage the latter. But experience shows that once the wages of a particular group go up, for whatever reason, this has a tendency

to spread to other areas. Raising the low paid, for example, is followed in due course by demands from the more skilled for a restoration of the traditional differentials. The market itself will tend in the same direction, since raising the costs to employers of the lower paid will make the more highly skilled relatively more attractive to hire at existing wages.

The problem of the low paid is one which, as we said, should be handled by additional training and education, and not by arbitrarily raising money wages through legislative fiat. Similar tendencies will occur when wages go up on account of productivity improvements. In that case the benefits from increased productivity should be allowed, as much as possible (a weasel phrase!), to show up in reduced prices, as they would do in the absence of union monopolization of the particular supply of labor, except of course for the rise needed to maintain or attract the necessary labor force. This latter factor may have been of significance in the coal industry in the United States, for example.

We will keep these tentative conclusions in mind as we survey experience in other countries.

THE NETHERLANDS

The experience of The Netherlands with incomes policies differs somewhat from that of the United Kingdom, partly because of the importance of external factors in the Dutch economy. While Britain was constrained by balance-of-payments considerations from time to time, in the Netherlands nearly half the gross national product is accounted for by exports. Consequently, it is of the utmost importance that Holland maintain its competitive position *vis-á-vis* the other international trading nations of the world. It is therefore not so surprising as it might be in other circumstances to find a willingness on the part of the Dutch trade unions and a socialist government to accept very stringent restraints on incomes. Dutch experience is significant not only for the degree of restraint that was accepted but also because of an experiment in gearing permitted wage increases to changes in productivity in particular sectors.

The Institutional Setting

Before exploring these experiences, we will review briefly the institutions involved with the setting of national wage policies. There are three major unions. Largest is the socialist oriented Netherlands Federation of Labor (NVV), followed closely by the Catholic Workers Union (NKV), and by the third but smaller Protestant Federation of Labor (CNV). These are organized vertically, duplicating each other's coverage of industrial lines, so that a particular plant or company might deal with all three unions. There is a similar division for employer associations, but the liberal nondenominational federation (CSMV) covers 80 percent of employers.

At the conclusion of World War II in 1945 there existed a strong feeling of solidarity and agreement between representatives of labor and the employers that cooperation was needed to repair the devastation of the war and to restore the country to a strong place in the world economy in the interest of maintaining full employment. In fact, toward the end of the war, representatives of the unions and the employers had met clandestinely to set up the Foundation of Labor with representatives from labor, employers, and the public.

Its function was to discuss wage policy jointly and to help formulate guidelines.

In 1945 a Central Planning Bureau was created to supply forecasts of employment, prices, and wages, the balance of payments, and domestic supplies for the year ahead. For this purpose, it used econometric models and discussed with the Foundation of Labor the implications of various incomes policies. It may be of interest that economists were strongly represented not only in the Central Planning Bureau but in the leadership of the trade union organizations as well. This may have contributed to the general agreement that a policy of wage restraint would contribute to enhancing the Netherlands's competitive position and would lead to high employment.

One other institution should be mentioned. This is the Board of Government Mediators which consulted with the Foundation of Labor but which was the government arm empowered to carry out the incomes policy and to intervene in particular disputes.

History

Despite the many factors working to restrain the rise in wages, it nevertheless seems surprising to this United States observer that wages for six years rose no faster than the cost of living index and in 1951 went up by only 5 percent while the cost of living rose 10 percent, implying a reduction in real wages. During this period, and into 1954, business accepted a strict price control whereby it agreed not to pass on wage increases in higher prices, though it was allowed to pass on increases in the cost of materials and other "external costs" (guilder for guilder). Since most materials were imported, this was a matter over which the country had little direct control.

This program can be labeled most successful in improving the Dutch balance of paymᵣnts. Also, unemployment was reduced to 3.2 percent by 1951. But because wages were rising no more rapidly than prices, labor was not in general sharing in the country's prosperity. Meanwhile, because productivity was increasing, the margin between wage costs and prices widened and profits rose. Labor increasingly expressed dissatisfaction with its lot under the controls and it wasn't long before the employers joined in. With profits high and employment tight, employers were anxious and willing to raise wages. In this situation a decision to allow wages to rise more rapidly than prices resulted in a wage explosion in 1954, with the official index up 16 percent, a figure that was matched again in 1956.

The wage rises of the middle fifties wound up in a balance-of-payments crisis in 1957, and a new program of restraint was accepted by the unions. This program was worked out by the Social and Economic Council, an organization set up in 1950 to supplement the Foundation of Labor. It had direct government representation as well as members from labor and the employers. However, despite endorsement by the union leaders, the membership of the unions refused to go along with the new program of restraint, perhaps because in the past the restraint had enhanced profits more than the welfare of wage earners.

Productivity Guideline

In 1959 a Liberal government came into power and, partly to satisfy the demands of employers who wanted more flexibility, put into effect what has perhaps become the most controversial feature of the Dutch experience with incomes policies. Prices were to stay the same, with some exceptions as will be noted later, except for a pass through (guilder for guilder) of nonwage-cost increases or decreases. In recognition that wages would need to rise more rapidly than prices to the extent of advances in productivity (output per manhour) if the distribution of income between wages and broadly-conceived profits was not to be altered, the policy was adopted of allowing wage increases to exceed price increases to the extent of the rise in productivity.

The unique feature of the Dutch productivity guidepost was that instead of gearing the rise in wages to the rise in overall productivity for the economy as a whole, as in the United States guidelines, wages were to follow productivity in particular sectors. To a degree this accorded with the need to get more people into the expanding industries which in general were those where productivity was growing more rapidly than average. It should be noted at this point that where productivity was growing exceptionally rapidly (no definition of this phrase was provided), an industry was expected to reduce prices rather than raise wages excessively. Conversely, in areas with little or no productivity growth, price increases would be condoned.

Two problems developed with the approach to basing wage changes on the change in sectoral productivity. The first problem was statistical in nature and involved the difficulty of determining just what the rise in productivity in a sector is. In practice, employers and the unions might agree on a wage settlement for a particular industry and then set about to develop the statistics on productivity in that sector needed to support the particular wage settlement. As anyone who has worked with numbers of this sort will attest, it is no simple job to say that such "contrived" numbers are right or wrong, expecially if one is trying to pinpoint by how much. In this sense, the exception for productivity gains is just like any other exception or loophole. Enough people will find a way to qualify for the exception so that in time it tends to become the rule.

This brings up the second difficulty with basing wage changes on sectoral productivity changes. It produces inequities. After all, why should a master electrician be paid more in an expanding than in a contracting industry if the job is the same on other counts? One can justify this within limits and for a time if it is necessary to funnel people into the expanding industry and out of the contracting one, but once a differential of this sort is opened up, a further widening of it will create a shortage of people in the industry which is contracting. In due course, then, employers can be counted on to point out this "inequity" even if the unions don't (and it's hard to imagine that they won't). So it will then be necessary for the lagging industry to "catch up" with wages in the expanding industry. This process can proceed rather rapidly in a full employment economy such as the Dutch one.

By 1963 the idea of sectoral productivity as a guide to wage changes was dropped. In its place, wage targets were to be set based on the Central Planning Bureau's econometric model. This merely substituted one impossible statistical problem for another. Based on its forecast (which was unbelievably bad!) there was an indicated need for wages to rise by 1.2 percent in 1963. Needless to say, this was so far from the realities of the situation at that time that it was openly flouted not only by labor but by employers as well. In fact, wages went up by 13 percent in 1963, 15 percent in 1964, and 14 percent in 1965.[49] This particular wage explosion did not bring on a balance of payments problem, but attempts were made to restrain it with "targets" of 6 percent for wage increases in 1966 and 7½ percent in 1967, supplemented by a price freeze in 1967. All were to no avail, and by 1968 all guidelines were abandoned.

Various attempts were made subsequently to hold down the rise of wages, but these appear to have had only a limited effect. The wage-price spiral continues apace.

Evaluation

What can we learn from the experience of the Netherlands? It is easy enough to shrug it off as just one more example of the failure of direct controls. From this we can go on to argue that controls are merely a delusion. They do no good and give policymakers a false sense of security, for in the end market forces will win out. Therefore, it can be argued, the only thing to do is to rely on monetary and fiscal policy, and if this means creating high unemployment for a long period to eliminate inflation and the excessive income gains that bring inflation about, so be it. There is no escaping it.

The above is an answer that may gratify academics. But we know it is an answer that the public will not accept at this juncture. The public wants both full employment and stable prices, and it wants them now. It is therefore up to us to explore further the possibility that some form of direct control, supplementing broad-scale monetary and fiscal policy, can play a part in restraining inflation within a framework of minimum unemployment.

In any case, it is not correct to say that incomes policy in the Netherlands has been an out-and-out failure, even though it wound up in repeated wage-price explosions and a resurgence of inflation. After all, free-market approaches had the same result. If anything, I believe it is fair to say that the incomes policy in Holland worked all too well. For it did succeed in holding down the rise in labor costs so well that it paid off in high employment, fast growth, and a strong external competitive position most of the time. But this did not mean that it could escape the consequences of excess demand from the outside. This excess demand pressure from abroad manifested itself in high profits in export industries and industries competitive with imports, which tended to expand at the expense of domestic industries, or at least at the expense of the domestic market and the standard of living of the average citizen. This is perhaps the real lesson of the Netherlands experience.

To summarize, the following seem to be the lessons to be learned from experience with incomes policies in the Netherlands:

1. It is impossible for a country heavily dependent on international trade to insulate itself from forces generated in the world market, at least so long as it maintains fixed rates of exchange with the rest of the world. If the country attempts to hold down its price and cost level below that of the rest of the world, this will of course have a beneficial effect on employment in the country, at least so long as others do not retaliate, and for a small country it can be expected that there will not be retaliation. But its very success in holding down costs and prices will mean that exports will expand, imports will lag, and much of the benefit from holding down prices will wind

up in the accumulation of foreign assets through a strong balance of payments surplus.

The foreign assets accumulated may wind up in the hands of the wealthy or of financial institutions, with very little accruing to the immediate satisfaction of the wants of the public. Also, profits in the export industries and those competitive with imports will rise. This creates what may be considered an inequity by raising the overall share of profits in the national income. In addition, it may lead to an unsustainable expansion of the export and import-competitive industries; unsustainable in the sense that it will tend to be reversed when the balance of payments reverts from strong surplus toward approximate balance. While most countries appear to wish to operate at a small surplus in their balance of payments (impossible, of course, for all countries) it is not likely that they will wish to continue forever to pile up larger and larger foreign exchange reserves through a continued balance of payments surplus.

2. The second lesson has to do with the experiment of setting the wage increase guideline for individual industries on the basis of productivity in that industry. Not only is this difficult statistically; the more important consequence is that it opens up an exception, a loophole, which in time becomes the rule. In a sense, the tail ultimately wags the dog, for if one industry is allowed to increase wages above the average, for whatever reason, this in time becomes the standard which others must emulate or catch up to, given of course a full employment economy.

3. It is helpful to have the force of law behind an incomes policy, as reflected in Holland's early postwar experience. But no law will stand without the support of

the public, as reflected in the wage explosions of the mid-1950s and the mid-1960s.

4. While a restraining monetary and fiscal policy is not a sufficient condition for attaining stability of the price level, it is a necessary one. Controls will not stop inflation without a good deal of help. In the early postwar years, while patriotic fervor was important, surely the existence of some slack in the labor market played a significant role in keeping the rise in wages down and keeping public support for the incomes policy in the interest of raising employment. Later, in the 1960s, with unemployment at 1 percent of the labor force or less, no amount of jawboning or legal restraints would suffice to hold back the market forces making for rising wages and prices. In addition to the demands of the unions, employers themselves were willing and anxious to pay higher wages and salaries to secure more workers, or to prevent the loss of the work force they had. So income controls, to be successful, must have the support of general monetary and fiscal policies to prevent too strong a demand pull.

NORWAY AND SWEDEN

We turn now to a review of the experience of Norway and Sweden with incomes policies, not so much from the standpoint of whether or not they worked, or why they failed to contain inflation, but because of the institutional arrangements that evolved. Both countries are characterized by strong organizations on both the employer and union sides. For example, members of the Swedish Employers Confederation (SAF) may not take a strike, initiate a lockout, or sign a contract without getting the approval of the Confederation. The labor organizations have similar strong powers.[50]

The end of World War II brought inflation as it did in all countries. The strong central collective bargaining associations on both sides, being somewhat jealous of their prerogatives and anxious to minimize the role of government in industrial relations, which had been solely the concern of the private parties since the turn of the century, took upon themselves the task of attempting to handle the inflation problem. For example, in Sweden, after wages had risen more than 8 percent in 1948, the Confederation of Swedish Trade Unions (LO) agreed to a voluntary wage freeze in 1949–50 during a balance-of-payments crisis. This broke down during the Korean War, when there was a wage explosion of more than 20 percent, but the central determination of what is known as "frame" wage agreements was resumed in 1956 and has continued to date.

In both Norway and Sweden the consideration of the overall frame agreements is made by the private parties but the government participates in an advisory capacity, in the sense of making economic forecasts for the period ahead and advising on the effects of different wage settlements for prices and the distribution of income. This is done in terms of a model of the economy, the Aukrust Model, developed in the late 1960s by Odd Aukrust of the Central Bureau of Statistics of Norway. This model evolved out of the frustrations of trying to reconcile inflation control with strong egalitarian precepts regarding the distribution of income.

The problem was this. If wages were controlled so as to keep prices of domestic goods and services reasonably stable, the result would be high profits in the internationally competitive industries and in those competing with imports. This happened in the Korean War period, for example, because prices of internationally traded commodities were determined on the world market, and were rising generally, while productivity was rising more rapidly in this area than in the field of domestic industries not subject to import competition. This meant that if wages were to be raised enough to keep the distribution of income in the internationally traded area unchanged, it would require a rise in wages in the domestic industries which would be higher than would be compatible with stable prices in those industries.

This meant, in nations as exposed to international economic influences as both Norway and Sweden were, that they had to address their economic policies generally, and income policies in particular, to maintaining their internationally competitive industries in a viable state, with sufficient but not excessive profits, which meant rising prices for commodities and services produced domestically. The alternative would have been to attempt to stabilize prices in the domestic sector by pursuing an appropriate policy on wages in those industries, but this would have allowed profits to increase too greatly in the internationally competitive industries. Of course, the latter alternative could only be considered a temporary solution because the higher profits in the internationally traded area would cause employers in those industries to try to attract workers from the domestic industries by offering higher wages and other benefits which would either draw workers into the export and import-competitive industries or raise wages and hence prices in the domestic industries beyond the guidelines.

This shows that it is virtually impossible for a small country, dependent on international trade for a large fraction of its national income (half or more in Scandinavia), to insulate itself from developments in the world market, at least so long as it wishes to maintain fixed exchange rates with other currencies. Accordingly, in Norway and Sweden policy is in effect directed to adjusting prices and income rates in the domestic economy so as to maintain equilibrium with developments in the international area.

The Aukrust Model

The Aukrust model was designed to facilitate analysis and policymaking to achieve the above result. It divides the economy into two groups of industries. One group is the "sheltered industries" which in turn are subdivided into agriculture and "other sheltered industries." Agriculture is treated separately because its income policy is negotiated separately. Services bulk large in the "other sheltered industries" group. The second group of industries is labeled "exposed industries" and includes import-competing manufactures, fisheries, shipping, and other export-oriented industries.

Simply put, the model assumes that prices in the exposed industries are given by international market conditions. Profits (or, more broadly, nonwage costs) in these industries would then be determined by the level of wages and productivity in those industries. Assuming a constant share of income for wages and profits, this means that wages would be determined once productivity was known. Once the wage increase is set for the exposed industries, a parallel increase will be made for the sheltered industries other than agriculture (determined separately).

The model in effect postulates a constant relationship between wage costs and prices for the sheltered industries, so given productivity change in the sheltered industries it is possible to predict prices in the sheltered industries (or to set a target for them under price control). Since productivity has risen more rapidly in the exposed industries than in the sheltered industries, and since prices determined in international markets have risen over the years, this means that inflation of prices is inevitable. For Norway, the increase in output per man-hour over the period 1951–67 was 4.5 to 5.5 percent per annum for the exposed industries and 2 to 2.5 percent per annum for the sheltered industries. The corresponding figures for Sweden over the period 1960–1967 were 7.5 percent and 3.6 percent, respectively.[51]

Within this framework, the government statistical services can offer factual data and forecasts on prices and productivity in the exposed industries, in particular, and the private parties can offer their own forecasts and interpretation of developments in these areas. Out of this can come an agreement between the employers and the unions over wage changes in the area of the exposed industries. This would presumably set the standard for the sheltered industries, implying some price increase in those industries.

Formulating the problem in this way points up the key significance of the export industries in the entire wage determination process. As Odd Aukrust put it for Norway:

with constant exchange rates, wages in the long run must adjust in a way which leaves the exposed industries "reasonably competitive."[52]

The Swedish Version

A more extensive discussion and analysis of the role of the export industries, and of the profitability of those industries, is contained in the joint report of the economists for the Swedish Confederation of Trade Unions, The Swedish Employers' Confederation, and the Swedish Central Organization of Salaried Employees, in which these economists suggested an Aukrust-type model for use in Sweden. Selected passages from this report follow:

It is however crucial that competitive ability be maintained in branches which do compete as exports, or with imported goods. This is an absolutely essential condition for the whole economy. Competitive ability depends on production costs as well as on quality and modernness. If production cannot be maintained at the forefront of technical development, it cannot in the long run be sold. Once investments are made, production and sales must take place, even if prices only cover variable costs. But no new investments, which operate to maintain competitive ability of production in the future, are made when profitability is low. Profitability in those firms which are dependent on the outside world has its influence on the international competitive ability of the economy via its influence on investments. The criterion of the international competitiveness of exports must thus be the behavior of investments. Competitive ability is thus not connected with a static model with given capital stock in the competitive sector, but rather with a cumulative, dynamic model in which not only profitability and scope for financing is included, but also subjective variables such as expectations and propensity to invest as well.[53]

* * * * *

. . . wages in the competitive sector cannot increase in the longer run beyond the room for them as determined by changes in productivity and prices without the profitability and competitive ability of these sectors *vis-á-vis* foreign production becoming insufficient in the longer run. At that time investments, exports and employment fall. The situation in the labor market becomes such that the rate of wage increase lessens.[54]

In other words, the exposed industries are those in which productivity is growing most rapidly (and presumably is also highest), and expansion of these industries offers the best hope for continued growth in the standard of living of wage earners as well as others in the future. Therefore it is imperative that these industries remain competitive with foreign producers, which they can do only if profits are maintained at a rate which will induce a sufficient flow of investment to keep them progressive, up-to-date, and hence competitive. Of course, it is a matter of debate as to just how high such profits should be, and no doubt labor economists and business economists might differ on this, particularly since too high a rate of profitability in the exposed industries will induce too much expansion in them. But it is rather remarkable that union and employer economists could agree so completely as to the wage strategy that a country like Sweden or Norway should attempt to follow in the interest of maximizing its present and future well-being. It would be constructive if we could get similar agreement among the professional representatives of the labor and employer sides in the United States.

From the foregoing, it is clear that the professional analysts felt that wage bargaining could significantly influence the distribution of income in the exposed industries as between wage-salary and other costs (profits in the gross sense). This follows from taking demand conditions in these industries as being determined by world forces beyond the control of the individual country. But it is of interest that this does not extend to the domestic or protected industries. Here the model assumes constancy in the relationship between wage-salary and other costs. As the three Swedish economists state it: "The distribution of income in the sheltered sector has been constant on the average during the period under investigation, 1960–67, even if it did fluctuate considerably within special areas."[55]

Given this dependence on the outside world, it will come as no surprise that neither Sweden nor Norway was able to resist the tide of inflation that swept the western world in the late 1960s. It culminated in those countries in a price freeze in 1971. The freeze was subject to considerable exceptions, including a pass-through of rises in import prices, so that prices actually rose. In this sense, as a means of controlling inflation, the incomes policy and the analytical framework within which in recent years it has been carried out, can be judged a failure. But then, for some time it has been recognized formally that Norway and Sweden cannot insulate themselves from price developments in the world market, at least so long as they maintain fixed exchange rates with other nations.

Evaluation

What can we learn from the experience of the Scandinavian nations and from the analytical model they developed to focus the central bargaining between the employer and union representatives? First, we see once again that foreign developments will swamp all efforts toward unilateral stabilization in a small country. The experience of Norway and Sweden was the same in the Korean War episode as that of Holland, i.e., a holdback of wages followed by a wage explosion induced by a demand-pull from abroad.

Second, the finding, in both Norway and Sweden, that

the distribution of income between profits and wages was virtually constant in the protected or domestic industries, is of great significance. It ties in directly with U.S. data on this point, which covers the whole economy, and supports our earlier conclusion that any attempt to raise the share of labor in the income distribution by raising wages is doomed to disappointment. Since in a reasonably free market wage costs and prices are inextricably linked together, a rise in wage rates beyond the room provided by rising productivity is bound to be reflected in time in a comparable rise in prices. The trick is to find a means to hold down the rise in wages and salaries, and prices will then take care of themselves. We will come back to this later.

There is one other finding that has widespread significance. This has to do with the relationships between wages in different industries in general, and the frustration of attempts to raise the wages of the low-paid relative to the average in particular. As to the first point, the Swedish economists say this:

. . . there seems to be a normal relation between the wage level of the competitive sector and that of the sheltered sector. . . . This relationship can be changed for individual years, but such a change immediately brings forces into being which tend to return the relation to its original position. . . . Our calculations of relative wages of the competitive and sheltered sectors demonstrate very considerable stability.[56]

On the relative wages of low-paid workers, notions of solidarity and egalitarianism are strong in both countries, especially in Norway. Both countries strove continuously to raise the level of wages of the low-paid. For a time this appeared to work, but the long-run forces of the market place seem to have kept customary differentials from narrowing greatly. As Ulman and Flanagan conclude:

Moreover, if it was indeed an LO objective to restrain general wage increases in order to create more "room" for raises for the low-paid workers, this result has not yet been appreciable. Comparisons of the relative wages of unskilled workers and of women, the two groups whose income positions the policy was particularly intended to improve, do not indicate much change, despite favorable treatment accorded in the centrally negotiated contracts.[57]

Analogous to the attempt to increase labor's share of the national income merely by raising money wages, the above experience suggests that attempting to raise the status of one group of workers relative to another may wind up by merely raising the general or average level of wages without altering the real relationship between different groups. To accomplish the objective of raising a particular group, the source of the differentials with other groups must be attacked directly, as through education, training, and the elimination of artificial discriminatory barriers, as against women, for example.

DENMARK

Denmark is similar to Norway and Sweden in being heavily dependent on foreign trade and in having strong organizations of labor and employers. As in Norway and Sweden, bargaining takes place centrally, with the Danish Federation of Trade Unions (LO) bargaining for the labor side and the Danish Employers' Confederation (DAF) representing industry. Moreover, the LO has maintained a "solidaristic" or egalitarian approach to bargaining, as the largest member of the Federation is a large union of unskilled workers (the DASF). Skilled workers are represented by about 71 craft unions. One might add parenthetically that the egalitarian aim is no more successful in Denmark than elsewhere. This is because the central negotiations only set minimum rates, and in local shop bargaining the traditional differentials tend to be restored.

Perhaps the most notable feature of Denmark's approach to anti-inflation policy in general, and incomes policy in particular, has been its unwillingness to accept an Aukrust-type model of its economy. The essential feature of such a model is that inflation is largely imported from outside in a small country dependent on world trade. Therefore, given fixed exchange rates, the best policy for such a country is to gear its stabilization efforts to staying even with the rate of inflation in industries entering into world trade and letting the domestic industries adjust their wages and prices accordingly. In such a model, inflation is imported from abroad. The Danes were not so sure that this was strictly true, at least for them. Rather, they thought the domestic industries might themselves be a source of inflation. The construction industry is singled out for particular attention in Denmark as initiating a wage pattern which then spreads by emulation to other industries.

Denmark is also interesting from our point of view because it did not consciously follow an incomes policy until 1962. Previously, it had followed classical policies of monetary and fiscal policy to restrain or encourage the expansion of the economy. However, in 1962, following two small balance-of-payments deficits in 1960 and 1961, and with a larger one looming for 1962, a law was passed setting up an Economic Council of 20 persons representing unions, employers, the civil service, agriculture and the handicraft industries, plus the Ministers of Finance and of Economics and a representative of the Danish National Bank. The Economic Council turned out to be largely a debating society, but the law that established it also provided for a three-man Board of Chairmen consisting of academic economists. This Board reacted immediately in 1962, as a 15 percent wage explosion was then in progress, with recommendations shortly enacted into law.

Legislation in February 1963 proclaimed a two-year freeze on wages, with some exceptions including a general increase of 2½ percent in the second year. It also provided for the distribution of 1½ percent of the total wage bill to the lowest paid. Further, it provided for the regulation of prices and profit margins and for a freeze on dividends and directors' fees. The Monopolies Board was to be notified of any price changes, and wage increases above the guidelines could not be counted as a basis for price increases. Foreshadowings of some of the later U.S. regulations can be seen here!

The freeze was effective in bringing down the rate of wage increases in 1963 and 1964. Increases in hourly earnings dropped from 12 percent in 1961 and 9.4 percent in 1962 to 8.7 percent in 1963 and 7.7 percent in 1964. By 1965, however, the increase was back up to 11.5 percent as shop stewards and plant managers together violated the legal restraints. Unemployment dropped in this time from 4.2 percent in 1963 to 2.4 percent in 1964 and to 2.0 percent in 1965.[58]

The government, at successive two-year intervals, suggested a 3 percent guideline for wage increases for the years 1965 through 1971, but this was virtually ignored,

156

and devaluation was necessary in late 1967. This was
followed by a partial freeze in 1963 by a newly-elected
conservative government; it was reimposed in 1970 temporarily. This experience is just one more bit of evidence
that direct controls will just not hold up in a situation of
strong excess demand.

FRANCE

The French experience is interesting primarily because
the unions in France represent no more than 20 to 30
percent of the labor force, and there is no real collective
bargaining in the tradition of the other nations considered so far. The unions are politically oriented in the
main, and this is especially true of the Communist-
dominated union, which is the largest and is represented
on the Commissariat du Plan, the central planning organization in France. The French economy is subject to a
high degree of central planning, at least for long-range
goals, and there is a good deal of mixed enterprise, in
the sense of industries having both private and government firms.

It is therefore of interest that France had a reasonably
good record on the price front until the three-week general strike of May–June 1968. Until then, inflation had
come largely in spurts—during the Korean War, in
1957–1958, and again in 1962–1963. From that time
prices drifted slowly upward at the consumer level until
the 1968 general strike set off a chain of wage and price
increases which has continued right down to date.

France did not in general try direct restraints on wages
and salaries, but relied from time to time on price controls in the hope that they would help to hold down

excessive income settlements. Price controls were imposed in 1952, and a period of stability in the consumer price index ensued until the controls were dismantled in late 1957. A freeze was instituted late in 1963 and was gradually eliminated for individual industries as they agreed to guidelines and a review of their pricing actions.

The Fifth Economic Development Plan, which covered the years 1966–70, did set forth specific guidelines for maintaining stable unit labor costs. In addition, the government attempted to set an example of restraint by holding down the wages of public employees. These norms were completely shattered in the settlement of the 1968 general strike, however. It is of interest that the wages which had been held down the most previously went up most in the strike settlement. Wages in manufacturing rose 11–13 percent, while those of the central government and nationalized industries went up 15–15½ percent, and for local government employees the increase was 19 percent.[59]

It would be tempting to conclude from this that reasonably full employment and stability of the price level are not incompatible objectives where collective bargaining is not a widespread practice, particularly as suggested by the experience of 1952–1957. However, the fact that France has such a high degree of central planning, a large amount of government enterprise, and also resorted to direct price controls during this period, makes it questionable to what extent such a conclusion is warranted, and in any case whether the French experience is at all applicable to the economy of the United States. Two things are clear, however. One is, again, that when demand becomes excessive controls will break down, even if it takes a social upheaval to do it, as in 1968. The second is, also once again, that trying to hold down one group of workers while others move ahead will ultimately be self-defeating, as the laggards will catch up to the leaders, assuming of course strong demand conditions.

WEST GERMANY

West Germany, in contrast to France, did not adopt price controls but tried to develop its incomes policy in terms of wage guidelines during the 1960s. By the beginning of the decade the surplus supply of labor in the form of unemployment and refugees from East Germany had been used up. Unemployment was at the 1 percent level through much of the 1960s except for a brief interruption in the recession of 1966–67.

There are 16 major unions in West Germany, organized along industrial lines, and encompassing about one third of the labor force. In addition, there is a federation of white collar unions covering another 8 to 10 percent of the labor force. These unions bargain largely at the regional or state level and are independent of the central federation, the Deutscher Gewerkschaftsbund (DGB). Local bargaining for pay is not usual, and the works councils in individual shops are not organs of the unions. In contrast, the employers are strongly organized. The central employers' association (BDA) even has a strike fund so that members may continue to pay fixed expenses and salaries of white collar workers during a strike.

Until the 1960s prices in West Germany had been relatively stable, and, until 1969 at least, the consumer price index increased less rapidly than in other countries. Nevertheless, there were some attempts to try to hold the growth of incomes and prices in line. The first of these was in 1960 when the president of the Bundesbank called for a guideline of 4 percent for wage increases in 1961, as this was expected to be the gain in productivity. The unions would not go along with this, stating that there should be price control and that labor should be permitted to increase its share of the national income. In fact, productivity rose some 6.4 percent in 1961, and this rather soured the unions on government forecasts generally.

In August 1963 a Council of Economic Experts, consisting of seven academicians, was established to analyse economic policies and present alternative policies for consideration. It was to make no recommendations itself, though of course it is difficult to avoid making implied recommendations in any analysis. In its first report at the beginning of 1965, the Council called for wage and price restraint and subsequently suggested norms for wage changes, which were generally above productivity change, to allow for tax and similar adjustments.

In the mid-1960s, also, there grew up the institution of "Concerted Action," whereby representatives of the government, employers, and unions meet together. Wage policy is discussed in very general terms, but the main thrust of the discussion in Concerted Action is toward general government policies relating to taxes, expenditures, and monetary policy.

This institutional background may have contributed to the relatively favorable price performance in Germany. Perhaps the most significant feature was the absence of a strong, militant union movement. However, some feel that the background fears of remembered inflation and serious unemployment were most influential in moderating labor's demands so that costs and prices were kept under good control. For example, in 1953 registered unemployment was 7.5 percent of the labor force.

By 1969, however, the recollection of past inflation and unemployment was apparently growing rather dim, and the young people in particular were anxious to take stronger action to improve their lot. As a result, in September 1969 a series of wildcat strikes ensued, directed often as much against the union leaders as against the employers. Given the strong demand situation, wage settlements, which had been running in the area of 5 to 7 percent per annum, were jumped up to 10 percent and more by the wildcat strikes. Needless to say, since 1969 West Germany has also joined the parade toward near-universal continuous inflation.

ITALY

Italy, less stable than West Germany politically, was nevertheless characterized by relatively stable prices in the 1950s and an absence of incomes policy restraints. There was an emergency freeze in 1946–1947, but no serious interest in incomes policy until 1963. As with Germany, there was a reserve of unemployed to draw upon, principally from the South, until the 1960s.

As in Germany, the unions were relatively weak in Italy. There are three major labor federations: the CGIL, affiliated with the Communist party; the CISL, affiliated with the Christian Democratic party; and, the UIL, allied with the Social Democratic party. These unions were more interested in achieving their aims through political means than through collective bargaining. However, the unions did make national agreements with the employers' federation, Confindustria. Since the members of Confindustria were mostly small businessmen, the agreements usually provided for minimum rates, differentiated by region (lowest in the South, though the differential gradually narrowed). The larger firms always paid above the minimum in response to varying demand conditions.

General demand-control policies, particularly monetary policy, were mainly relied upon for controlling the economy. An interesting feature of the labor agreements was a cost-of-living escalator under which wages went up 0.6 percent for each 1.0 percent increase in the consumer price index. In the third quarter of 1961, in the midst of a boom in industrial production and with unemployment down to 3 percent, a wage explosion began and wages went up one third in the next two years. Credit was then restricted and a recession ensued in 1964. But prices kept going up. This was attributed to a sudden pushfulness on the part of the unions, which were then turning their interest to collective bargaining.

In an effort to stem the inflation tide, the government prevailed upon the unions to postpone the reopening of their contracts in 1965. The business recovery that ensued was in fact marked by a high degree of price stability, again until 1969. There was an attempt to include a wage-policy guideline in the five-year development plan for 1966–70, but the unions were far from enthusiastic about this so it was not stressed—in fact, it was even suggested in the plan that wage increases might promote the growth of productivity.

In any case, 1969 witnessed what has been called "the hot autumn." Wages went up 16 percent in 1970, accompanied by considerable political disequilibrium and fear of possible revolution. Italy, too, now continues on an

162

inflationary course despite the fact that it, like others in Western Europe, underwent a recession in 1970–71.

CONCLUSIONS FROM EUROPEAN EXPERIENCE

Let us now summarize the conclusions we can reach as to conditions most likely to contribute to the success of any incomes policy, based on our brief examination of the postwar experience of the Western European countries.

Public Support Needed

The first requisite is a rather general one, namely, broad public support for any program. Without such support, no program will survive. In the immediate postwar years there seems to have been strong support for programs of restraint in wage settlements and in prices, based on the conclusion among all classes of society in each country that this was necessary to restore the health of that country's economy generally, and the strength of its international competitive position in particular. The Dutch willingness to accept wage increases no greater than the rise in the cost of living is illustrative, if somewhat extreme.

With the passage of time, growing affluence, and perhaps through experience with wage hold-downs which led to profit explosions, leading in turn to wage explosions, the incentive to restrain income demands became less pressing. Also, in Germany and Italy in particular, the fading into the background of the recollection of heavy unemployment and inflation caused the labor unions to press more strongly for their objectives through collective bargaining.

This experience suggests that popular support for incomes policies must be founded on something more fundamental than an appeal to international competitive ability and righting the balance of payments. This is because righting the balance of payments may well result in a socially unacceptable division of the social product as between wages and salaries on the one hand and profits, in the gross sense of nonwage costs, on the other. Profits explosions of this character were most notable in the Korean War period in the smaller countries such as the Netherlands and Scandinavia.

However, while substantial fluctuations in gross income shares may accompany income restraints in countries heavily dependent on external trade and which keep exchange rates fixed with other countries, this is not a necessary feature of income restraints in large countries such as the United States. In fact, the whole idea of holding down incomes is that this will hold down prices. This will come about through holding down costs and also holding down the purchasing power which otherwise would be available to pay the higher prices. Such interaction between costs, purchasing power, and prices is undoubtedly a significant factor in the observed long-run tendency toward constancy of the relation between prices and wage and salary costs per unit, which we loosely call "labor" costs. This was observed in the experience of the United States and also in Norway and Sweden for the domestic or "protected" industries producing exclusively or primarily for the home market. With the U.S. having such a small percentage of its GNP in foreign trade (exports 6.3 percent of GNP in 1971) it is to be expected that the constancy of the relationship between labor costs and prices would show up in the overall statistics for the economy, as it does, and not just in the domestic industries alone, for which we do not have separate statistics.

The constancy over time in the labor-profit shares in GNP is important in evaluating another cause of breakdown in incomes policies and the relationship of this to the kind of public understanding and support needed. Breakdown of the controls comes about through the attempt to increase the share of one group or another. Usually this is triggered by some particular union demand which, if it is granted, then spreads to other unions; or it may come by attempting to raise the share of a particular segment of the population, such as the low paid. As we have seen, such attempts usually wind up ultimately with other groups being adjusted upward to the one getting the increase.

For the sake of completeness, we hasten to observe that an increase for one group need not spread to other groups immediately. In fact, the lag can be quite substantial if industry is operating below capacity and there is a measure of unemployment in the labor force. It is not likely, however, that this will be the long-run outcome under conditions of full employment. With full employment, employers will find it to their advantage to attempt to economize on the use of labor whose wage has risen and increase their use of labor whose wage has lagged behind. Since such wage increases are either set by union contract or by legislation (for example, the minimum wage) the action of employers will bid up the wages of the lagging group.

Something of this sort appears to have happened in the United States in the 1960s. Union wages would first go up more rapidly than nonunion wages in a period of unemployment, and then as activity rose, nonunion wages would tend to gain more rapidly, eventually catching up to the rise for union wages. Over a period the two apparently tended to equalize. Thus the initial upratchet of union wages spread through demand-pull which equalized the nonunion to the union level until a new round started again. Theoretically, this process could be inhibited if the public would be willing to tolerate a level of unemployment high enough to keep the nonunion wages from catching up with the union wages. But it is doubtful that the public would tolerate such a high rate of unemployment for long.

For the sake of still further completeness, we must admit that there is no theoretical reason why the ratcheting upward of incomes and prices couldn't start from the profits side. Industry in general might just raise prices in an effort to increase profits generally. Such concerted action strains the bounds of credulity, but it is conceivable that one industry might get the idea that for one reason or another it should raise its prices, then others might follow. The steel industry comes to mind as a possible—some would say plausible—case of an initiator of price increases which others might follow. But if this were to happen without any other changes taking place (in particular in the absence of a general wage increase) the higher prices would lead to a lower volume of sales, and output would be curtailed, as appears to have happened in the 1930s, for example, with the NRA codes. This would then lead to unemployment, followed in turn by expansionary monetary and fiscal policies, which would lead to expanded sales and a bidding up of the price of labor to match the rise in profit rates. In the end, the shares of profits and of wages and salaries would be the same as before, but wages, profits, and prices would all have been marked up in money terms, and all by the same proportion in the absence of any other changes.

The reader can reach his own conclusion as to how the expansionary process might get started. My own view is that profit inflation as the initiating factor is most unlikely to be significant under most circumstances—unless it should be government inspired, as in the case of NRA cited above. It is much more likely to come from the side of labor, usually in the form of a union demand, although legislative enactments, such as a rise in the minimum wage, could also play a significant part. The problem is that such demands may have the sympathy and support of the public, and of the public's representatives in Congress, because of the public's apparent belief that it is possible to improve the lot of labor by raising wages.

This brings up the point that, if any incomes policy is to have a chance of acceptance as part of a long-run approach to controlling inflation, it must be grounded in a public understanding that holding down the growth of incomes in general, and particularly the growth of wage incomes since these make up the bulk of total incomes, will in fact hold down the price level and will not result merely in a rise in the share of the national product going to profits. On the negative side, the public must understand that increasing wage rates will not succeed in raising the share of wages in the national income, but will merely raise the price level compared to what it would be in the absence of the wage increase. Further, it is possible to hold down prices in the long run *only* if the rise in incomes is restrained.

Of course, it is possible to raise the level of any particular group of wage-earners, such as the teamsters, the steelworkers, or the autoworkers, without causing an immediate proportionate increase in the *general* price level, as distinct from the prices of trucking services, steel, or automobiles. So in this sense one group of wage earners can increase its share of the national income, but this will be primarily at the expense of other wage earners whose wages do not go up, and who must pay the higher costs for trucking services, steel, or automobiles.

Only if the above proposition in elementary economics is understood and accepted by the public, is there reason to believe that a form of incomes policy might be worked out which would have some chance of succeeding in the long run as part of a general program to bring the price level under control. This indicates that educators and leaders of public opinion generally have a special obligation to bring this particular truth to the public. Political leaders, also, should be careful of the extent to which they cater to popular prejudice in seeking solutions to problems of public irritation and aspiration. There is no free lunch—one cannot eat what hasn't been produced. This is obvious but not always recognized, or more particularly there is an exaggerated notion of the extent to which we can get Joe, the other fellow, to pay for our lunch.

General Controls Also Needed

Assuming there is a broad understanding that controlling incomes will in fact control prices, and that only controlling incomes will do so in the long run, experience suggests a number of other points that must be considered if we are to be successful in finding a program which will keep inflation under control. One is a recognition that direct controls of prices and wages will not themselves do the trick. It is necessary to bring overall demand under control through appropriate monetary and fiscal policies. In other words, too-full employment will break down controls by causing employers to bid up the price of labor in an attempt to expand their work forces, or to hold them together against the inroads of other employers. This then becomes a typical demand-engendered wage-price spiral.

It is difficult to say just what level of employment would be excessive in this sense, assuming a viable policy of income restraint were in effect. One could guess that it should be possible to approach a 97 percent employment rate in the United States, and possibly higher in the course of time, as we suggested earlier. Other nations, assuming stability of exchange rates as a goal of policy, would have a special incentive to restrain incomes in order to keep their international competitiveness. They might therefore be able to press the employment rate upward still higher without generating a general scramble by employers to raise wages and salaries.

General Freeze Accepted—But Not a Solution

Another lesson learned from experience abroad is that the best-accepted and most widely-observed control is the general freeze. It is simple to understand and can be readily seen to be a clear interruption to any wage-price spiral which may have been in effect before the freeze. However, there is one thing about freezes—not one has lasted very long. Hence the general freeze cannot be looked upon as a long-run solution to the problem, necessary as it may be to interrupt a spiral under way. This is because any freeze will catch some wages, salaries, or prices in an inappropriate situation, with either wages or prices out of line for temporary reasons within a general equilibrium of supply and demand. With respect to prices, this would include situations where there is either a temporary shortage or surplus of supply, and in the case of wages or salaries it might include some workers who had not caught up with the most recent "round" of increases.

This means that after a brief period under a freeze, it becomes necessary to provide for exceptions and adjustments. At first these are needed to correct special situations or inequities of the kind mentioned above. But as time goes on, the original pattern of wage and price relationships becomes more and more inappropriate to changing conditions. This means that more and more exceptions will be necessary. To such exceptions may well be added, if the experience of others is a guide, a general sympathy and desire to raise the wages of the low paid, or to allow bigger than standard wage and salary increases for industries or firms with above-average productivity growth. As we observed, this can mark the beginning of the end of the control system.

Controls Must Be Integrated with Market System

Well, then, one asks, what *are* the standards one can apply to the adjustment of individual prices and wage and salary rates? What *is* the rule that will govern them? The answer is that *no* rule or set of standards, *no* administrative machinery, is capable of handling the innumerable decisions that must be made in a modern economy. In an economy of limited choices—one with barely enough resources, for example, to provide a minimum of food, clothing, and shelter; or in wartime when the civilian economy is frozen in the interest of focusing all energies on the war effort—it is conceivable that price and production decisions could be centrally planned for some period of time. But that it could be done in a modern peacetime economy where choices seem to be widening in geometric fashion, is utterly inconceivable except for relatively short periods.

Hence we are thrown back on the market mechanism as the only practical method of ordering production in the long run. This means that prices and wages and salaries must be allowed to fluctuate relative to each other. Only in this fashion can production and distribution respond over time to changes in consumer demands, to advances in technology in different fields, to the changing availability of energy sources and raw materials, and to the changing preferences of workers as to the lines of endeavor they would like to pursue.

How can these needs for a successful program be reconciled? On the face of it they are diametrically opposed. On the one hand, we must have rules that are unequivocal, to which there will be few exceptions, or better yet, none at all; and on the other hand, the control system must be flexible or it cannot possibly avoid interfering with the normal efficiency with which the price system directs resources to the production of goods and services that consumers want most. This is essentially the rock on which control systems in the past have foundered. Accordingly, it seems premature to attempt to suggest a solution until we complete our review of U.S. experience with the Nixon administration's New Economic Policy dating from August 15, 1971. Suffice it to say that the need for flexibility is a point about which we must be concerned in evaluating the U.S. system and anticipating possible changes if it is to evolve into a long-run mechanism. We believe there is an answer.

Participation and Legal Enforcement

There are two other features of an ideal control plan that the experience of others suggests would be desirable. One is that the control machinery should have the support, or at least the tolerance, of the organized parties to the major collective bargaining decisions of the nation. This is a major feature of the structure for implementing incomes policies in the Scandinavian countries, it will be recalled. In the United Kingdom, on the other hand, the unwillingness of the Trade Union Congress to go along with income restraints under Conservative governments has been a major hindrance to their effectiveness. Finally, having the income restraints backed by the force of law, with penalties for violations, would appear to help insure their success.

These then are our tentative conclusions as to the requisites for success in a controls program in the long run:

1. There must be wide public support, grounded in a sophisticated understanding of the relation between incomes and prices.
2. The program must be supported by a control of demand through monetary and fiscal policies.
3. There should be a minimum of exceptions which might in time become the rule.

4. The program should be flexible so that it can accommodate itself to changing circumstances.
5. The major labor groups should participate in the machinery to implement the program, and this machinery should have the force of law.

7

Direct Controls: The New Economic Policy of the United States

WE TURN now to the recent U.S. experience with wage and price controls, starting from August 15, 1971. Our objective is to seek out the lessons it holds for developing a mechanism of general and specific controls that might serve with only slight modification thereafter to maintain both full employment and price stability.

We will observe at the outset that the U.S. policymakers apparently learned a good deal from the experience of others with incomes policies and tried to avoid some of their mistakes. The venture into direct controls followed the well-worn trail of imposing a wage-price freeze by executive order.

BACKGROUND TO THE DECISION FOR CONTROLS

The decision to try direct controls followed a period of growing public disenchantment with the policy of try-

173

ing to control inflation with a policy of overall demand restraint through fiscal and monetary restriction alone. While the period of demand restraint was begun in 1969 and continued into 1970, it was never contemplated that it would be allowed to run into an outright recession. The fact that it did was thanks in part to the General Motors strike in 1970. The National Bureau of Economic Research has labeled the period from November 1969 to November 1970 a "contraction," to use their terminology, or what we usually call a recession. Moreover, the period from November 1970 to mid-1971 was one of very halting recovery at best. The Federal Reserve Board Index of Industrial Production recovered from the General Motors strike low of 102.8 in November 1970 to 106.0 by February 1971 (1967 = 100), but rose only another 1.4 points by June and then began to slack off.

Equally important, wage and benefit decisions were continuing to provide for compensation increases substantially in excess of productivity growth, in fact or in prospect, and first-year settlements in particular were tending to grow. Also, prices in the key sector of industrial wholesale prices were beginning to rise at an accelerating rate in the summer of 1971. For example, the BLS Index of Wholesale Prices of Industrial Commodities jumped .6 percent in July and another .5 percent in August (mostly before the freeze), so some action was called for. The policy of pure demand restraint alone was bankrupt.

The freeze was for 90 days and was part of a package of actions labeled the New Economic Policy. The other two parts consisted of allowing the dollar to float in exchange markets along with the imposition of a 10 percent surcharge on imports. Finally, there was a program in the tax field reducing taxes to stimulate demand and encourage expansion. Our concern at this point will be with the control program.

THE CONTROL SYSTEM

Perhaps drawing on the experience of others, only a temporary freeze was provided for—90 days—to be followed by something else, which has since been labeled Phase II. The order creating the freeze and providing for its expiration on November 13, 1971, also set up the Cost of Living Council. This body consisted of Cabinet officers and other high government officials and was charged with the responsibility of fixing overall goals for the program and of setting up the machinery for controls to follow the freeze. This resulted in the creation of two other bodies, the Pay Board and the Price Commission, both essentially public bodies under the Cost of Living Council.

The Pay Board consisted of 15 members, five each from industry, labor, and the public. In late March, however, four of the labor members withdrew and the Board was reduced to 7 members, including the one labor member who did not withdraw, one of the industry members, and the five public members, including the Chairman, George H. Boldt, though all them became public members. The Price Commission consisted entirely of public members and had responsibility for prices and rents. In addition there were some advisory committees: on interest and dividends, state and local government cooperation, health services, a retail advisory committee, and an executive compensation subcommittee.

The previously-existing Construction Industry Stabilization Commission was placed under the Pay Board, and the National Commission on Productivity continued to be responsible for developing and promoting measures to increase productivity.

THE PAY STANDARDS

The Cost of Living Council set an overall goal for the Phase II program, following the freeze, of reducing the rate of price increase to between 2 and 3 percent by the end of 1972, or about half the rate before the freeze. The Pay Board used this overall goal as the starting point for formulating its standard for pay increases. This was set at 5½ percent, which assumed productivity increases of 3 percent per annum, representing the long-run trend increase in output per man-hour, and allowing 2½ percent for price increases. By implication this assumed that the division of the product between profits in the gross sense and wages and salaries would remain essentially unchanged.

The Pay Board allowed certain exceptions to this general standard. First, it approved certain contracts initially at rates above 10 percent for initial annual increases. This included the coal contract which had been signed during the freeze period and before November 14, 1971, when the Phase II controls became effective. The railroad signalmen's contract approval was influenced by the fact that part of the increase had been legislated by the Congress. The Board also approved an increase averaging 13 percent for the dockworkers on the West Coast, the East Coast, and the Gulf Coast. While this was above the guideline, it was a substantial reduction from the settlement negotiated by the parties themselves.

During Phase II, the Pay Board also allowed the payment retroactively of wage increases which had been held up during the freeze. This was required by the terms of the extension of the Economic Stabilization Act of 1970 to April 1973.

A number of general exceptions were also permitted. These included outright exemptions for adjustments in Federal pay rates and those required by the Fair Labor Standards Act. Also, pay increases of up to 7 percent would be permitted: (1) if needed to attract or retain essential employees for whom the firm had a significant number of vacancies, (2) if needed to maintain historical tandem relationships with other firms or industries, (3) if increases during the previous three years totaled less than an average of 7 percent per annum, and (4) similarly for certain cost-of-living adjustments. In addition, the amendments extending the ESA to April 1973 provided that wage increases to any individual whose earnings were substandard or who was a member of the working poor were not to be limited in any manner, nor were employer contributions to benefit plans, unless they were "unreasonably inconsistent" with the general standards for wages, salaries, and prices. The "unreasonably inconsistent" qualification also applied to the retroactive payment of wages provided by contracts as alluded to above.

PRICE CONTROLS

The Price Commission took the midpoint of the Cost of Living Council goal of a 2 to 3 percent increase by the end of 1972 and announced that it would aim to hold the increase in prices for the economy to no more than 2½ percent per year. To implement this goal, it announced that price increases beyond the level established in the freeze would be permitted only in accordance with its regulatory standards. These provided for raising prices by the percentage by which allowable cost increases exceeded productivity gains for the industry in which the firm was located, as determined by the Department of Labor. Allowable increases with respect to wages and salaries included only the amount which accorded with the Pay Board's basic standard of 5½ percent per annum, even if a larger increase had been allowed by the Pay Board. This is an example of the generally "tough" stance that the Price Commission took in interpreting its responsibilities under the Economic Stabilization Act.

There was a margin limitation on the amount by which a firm might increase prices. Such increases were not to raise the firm's margin of profits before taxes as a percentage of sales above the margin in a base period, the base period being the average of the two best years of the firm's most recent three fiscal years ending before August 15, 1971. However, there was no limit on the dollar total of profits.

Special provisions governed rents, insurance, health services, fees, and other charges by state and local and federal governments, and seasonal price fluctuations. These were to be in general conformity with the overall 2½ percent price increase limitation. Dividends were subject to a voluntary 4 percent increase in the amount paid per share (with appropriate adjustments for stock splits and stock dividends) over the largest amount paid in fiscal 1969, 1970, and 1971, or in calendar 1971. Finally, firms incurring losses were allowed to raise prices to the break-even level, and firms with sales of $1 million or less were allowed to increase prices to bring their profits up to 3 percent of sales. Also, interest rates remained uncontrolled, though subject to surveillance by the Committee on Interest and Dividends of the Cost of Living Council. Finally, raw agricultural and raw seafood products were exempted from control.

THE THREE TIERS

To aid in the enforcement of the price and compensation regulations, a system of approvals and reporting was devised under which firms were divided into three categories, or tiers. Tier I included firms with sales of $100 million or more when requesting a price increase or with 5,000 or more workers affected by a requested wage increase. Tier I covered about 1,500 firms with 45 percent of all sales and about 10 percent of all employees. These firms were required to obtain prior approval for pay or price increases, except to the extent that price increases might be covered under term limit pricing arrangements. These arrangements were negotiated individually and limited the overall rise in prices for a particular concern but allowed some flexibility for individual items. Tier I firms also were required to submit quarterly reports on prices, costs, and profits to the Price Commission.

Tier II firms were those for which price increases would affect sales of $50 million and wage increases would involve 1,000 to 5,000 workers. This covered about 1,000 firms with 5 percent of all sales and 7 percent of all employees. These firms were required to report price or pay changes but did not need to obtain advance approval. They also filed quarterly reports with the Price Commission on prices, costs, and profits.

Tier III firms were exempt from notification or reporting requirements, but were expected to follow Price Commission and Pay Board regulations and were subject to surveillance and spot checks. Tier III included all firms not included in Tier I or Tier II, estimated to represent some 10 million firms with 50 percent of all sales and 83 percent of all employees.

EXPERIENCE UNDER FREEZE AND PHASE II

A favorable interpretation was placed, at least by the Nixon administration economists, on experience under the freeze from mid-August to mid-November 1971 and under Phase II from mid-November 1971 to early January 1973. Not that inflation was stopped, or met the objective of an inflation rate of 2½ percent per year. The increase in the Consumer Price Index for 1972 was 3.4 percent, computed from December 1971 to December 1972. This was the same as for 1971, which was influenced by the August-November freeze, but compared quite favorably with increases of 5.5 percent for 1970 and 6.1 percent for 1969.

The above-indicated average experience for full years masks to some extent the improvement that apparently was made in reducing inflation in the latter part of the Phase II period. At least, the Council of Economic Advisers found it worthwhile to note in its January 1973 *Report* that the Consumer Price Index rose at an annual rate of 1.9 percent during the freeze, and at 4.8 percent during the expected bulge from November 1971 to February 1972, the initial period of Phase II; but that from February 1972 to December 1972 the rate of rise fell to 3.0 percent.[60]

Similar gratification was derived from the trend of

wage payments. The Council noted that the Department of Labor's measure of average hourly earnings for the private nonfarm economy, which is adjusted to eliminate the effects of overtime and interindustry shifts, was up by 6.9 percent in each of the two twelve-month periods preceding the August 1971 freeze. The rate per annum dropped to 3.1 percent during the freeze, rose to 9.5 percent in the immediate post-freeze bulge, but dropped off to a rate of 5.6 percent in the period from February to December 1972.[61]

The Council was cautious about attributing the moderation in price and pay increases to the controls. It might have occurred in any case. However, the Council clearly believed that the controls had substantially reduced the risk that inflation would accelerate. As it concluded:

The goal of policy in 1971 and 1972, as we have pointed out, was not only to reduce the probable rate of inflation but also to reduce the general fear of continued or rising inflation and thus to increase confidence in the achievement of price stability. A change in the perception of the U.S. inflation problem has taken place. The controls have made a substantial contribution to this.[62]

In support of its conclusion that there had been a substantial decline in the expectation of inflation, the Council cited public opinion surveys, an apparent growing confidence on the part of foreigners in the stability of the U.S. as reflected in their willingness to hold increasing amounts of dollars, and finally a decline in interest rates in 1972, which it felt could only happen in a period of economic expansion if there had been a decline in the expectation of inflation.[63]

Thus one can imagine that it was fairly easy for the Council to convince itself that the climate was favorable for easing controls. In addition, evidence was accumulating that the controls were beginning to create shortages and inefficiencies. These were in only a few areas but it was feared that the problem would spread as the economy as a whole would begin to bump against capacity ceilings in 1973.

Most of the evidence of waste and inefficiency from the Phase II controls program came from the lumber and plywood industry, where demand was booming. It was reported that production was being held back to avoid violating the profit margin limitations. Standard cuts of lumber were being modified to create "new products" which were exempt from controls. It was also reported that carloads of lumber were being shipped around the country from one dealer to another, accumulating markups, before reaching the ultimate user.

In petroleum refining, setting the ceiling prices at the August 1971 levels, which were relatively favorable to the production of gasoline, created a disincentive to produce fuel oil for the winter. Further, the rise in economic activity abroad was making it increasingly attractive in many lines to sell abroad rather than at ceiling prices in the domestic market.[64]

The Council did note that farm product prices had been rising because of adverse weather at home and increasing demand from abroad, both of which contributed to a reduction in supplies available for the U.S. market. The rise in foreign demand reflected adverse weather abroad as well as rising incomes.

The growing indications of specific shortages and inefficiencies induced by the price controls were perhaps inconsistent with the conclusion that the overall expectation of inflation had moderated, though admittedly that observation is made with the benefit of hindsight. In any event, they formed the background against which the disastrously inflationary events of 1973 and 1974 unfolded. These events began with an initial relaxation of controls (Phase III), followed by the reimposition of a freeze, followed in turn by a Phase IV similar to Phase II, and ending with the complete abandonment of all controls as of April 30, 1974, except for the dragging out over a longer period of pricing agreements entered into in the phase-out period of late 1973 and early 1974, and the continuation of controls on energy.

The events of 1973–74 will be described in the next chapter, where we will also draw conclusions from the entire experience of August 1971 through April 1974 as to the role controls can and cannot play as part of an overall program to bring inflation down in the future.

8

1973–74: Phases III, IV, and Out

A SEPARATE chapter is warranted by the events of 1973 and 1974 up to the expiration on April 30, 1974, of all controls except in the area of energy. This period witnessed a series of events which it would be difficult to imagine in fiction, and which in combination culminated in double-digit inflation in most of the western world and most particularly in the United States. The period offers invaluable testimony to the contribution direct controls can and cannot make to an overall program aimed at stabilizing the price level under conditions approaching full employment.

OVERVIEW

The events which contributed to the inflation debacle included: (1) a simultaneous boom in all countries world-

184

wide; (2) an unusual coincidence of short crops in all nations—reinforced, as fate would have it, by the sudden disappearance of anchovies off the Peruvian coast; (3) a decision by the oil producing nations of the Middle East to cut production and triple the price of crude oil; and (4) through it all, for the United States, the pervasive price-raising effects domestically of the devaluation of the dollar, especially from August 1971 when the dollar was allowed to float downward against other currencies.

It is difficult, at least at this point in time, to assess accurately the relative contribution of each of the four items listed to the inflationary blow-up. Some might attribute it primarily to prior excessive monetary and fiscal expansion. It is true that growth of the money stock rose from 6.3 percent in 1971 to 8.7 percent in 1972, based on December to December changes.[65] Also, the high employment budget of the federal government was shifted from a surplus of $400 million in calendar 1971 to a deficit of $5 billion in calendar 1972, though the actual deficit was declining in this period under the stimulus of rising business activity.[66]

There can be no question that these monetary-fiscal measures were stimulative. But that they alone accounted for the explosiveness of the 1973–74 inflation is open to serious question. I noted previously that the Council of Economic Advisers was convinced that underlying inflationary trends had been subdued sufficiently so that it was ready to recommend the relaxation of Phase II controls. The Council was not alone, however, in its sanguine view of the prospects for inflation. Economic forecasters were generally optimistic. The estimates of 8 econometric models and 25 individual economists, including the author, whose forecasts were available late in 1972, ranged from 2.6 to 4.1 percent for the increase in the GNP deflator for 1973, or well below the actual of 5.4 percent.[67] Given the time lags between monetary-fiscal developments and economic activity, one would think that at least one observer would have been able to foresee the 1973 inflation if it had been due solely to monetary-fiscal forces.

It seems safe to conclude that all of the factors listed played a part in the 1973–74 inflation breakout. Nevertheless, in retrospect, and given the crop failures and the petroleum shortage, it now seems that the monetary-fiscal expansion was overdone. It furnished a receptive environment for the price increases induced by the crop failures and petroleum holdup.

DEVALUATION'S CONTRIBUTION

Comment seems in order about the dollar devaluation because its contribution to the inflationary picture came as something of a surprise. The devaluation, as measured against a trade-weighted average of 14 currencies, reached more than 20 percent by the summer of 1973 in relation to a May 1970 base, according to calculations by Morgan Guaranty Trust Company. Somewhat less than half occurred up to the time of the Smithsonian agreement in December 1971, and the balance after that.[68]

In part, and probably in large part, the devaluations were a recognition of a previous overvaluation of the dollar which had developed progressively in the postwar years—and this was not a surprise. Nevertheless, the devaluations also made a positive contribution to the price-raising forces already present in the U.S. economy

—and the extent of this contribution was a surprise to most observers.

The devaluations contributed to inflation in the United States in several ways. First, the cost of U.S. exports to foreign users was reduced at a time when their economies were expanding. They responded by increasing their purchases of U.S. exports, thereby tending to raise prices in dollars directly and also indirectly by reducing supplies available to the U.S. market. This was most evident in foodstuffs, but occurred also in other commodities.

Devaluation also raised the cost of imports to U.S. users. Ordinarily this might have been expected to hold down or even reduce the rise in prices abroad, and of course there was a tendency in that direction. However, business was expanding so much everywhere that this tendency was swamped and prices went up in all countries. Rising prices of both exports and imports tended to spread to items competing with either one in the domestic market, such as in steel, autos, paper, and chemicals, for example. Since prices of many of these were held down by price controls, increasing quantities tended to be diverted to foreign markets and were not available for use in the United States.

From this episode it became clear that it is no longer possible for the United States to ignore world developments in formulating its economic policies. The rest of the world can have a profound impact on U.S. developments. At the same time, having accomplished the devaluations and the painful adjustments they required in our price level and living standards, we are now in a favorable position to implement a policy of bringing down inflation in the United States without threatening to create recession in the rest of the world. With floating exchange rates, a reduction in inflation in the United States which is not matched abroad can be reflected in an appreciation of the dollar and need not cause rising unemployment in other countries. Such unemployment might tend to occur if, with fixed exchange rates, foreign nations were compelled to take deflationary actions to combat unfavorable balances of trade or payments.

Now that the adjustment to floating rates has been made, the United States is in a position to lead in the battle against inflation by adopting policies appropriate to solving the problem within the constraints of its own institutional framework. Other nations can then follow along as their own circumstances make possible and appropriate.

NO WAGE PUSH

The reader may have observed that we have not included a push from rising wage and salary costs as a factor in the recent inflation. This is because, on the positive side, the supply and demand factors enumerated seem quite sufficient by themselves to account for the inflation. On the negative side, there is just no indication that rising wage costs were pushing up prices significantly— quite the contrary, in fact. In the field of manufactured commodities, for example, prices rose progressively relative to labor costs. The price index for such commodities rose from 120.7 in December 1972 to 149.2 in April 1974, or by 23.6 percent. The index of unit labor costs for manufactured commodities rose over the same period from 118.3 to 128.1, or by only 8.3 percent.[69] The push on manufactured goods prices came not from labor costs but from raw materials, reflecting the demand and supply forces summarized previously.

This does *not* mean, we hasten to add, that labor costs are unimportant in the current environment—only that other factors were responsible for the degree of inflation witnessed in 1973–74. Since these other factors were all presumably of a nonrecurring nature, one can hope that as they pass into history the rate of inflation will subside to a basic long-run upward creep. It is this long-run upward creep to which this book is mainly addressed, and the trend of labor costs is definitely related to it. But before going into this more extensively, let us first turn to a more detailed review of developments in 1973–74 as they pertain to the controls system.

THE PHASE III DISASTER

On January 11, 1973, the Administration announced Phase III of the controls program. This provided for an easing of requirements for advance notification and some modification of the rules covering the profit margin limitation, but in general the standards remained the same as in Phase II for both wages and prices. As previously, prices could be increased only to reflect cost increases. However, if a firm's prices did not increase on average by more than 1½ percent in a year its profit margin would not be limited. This was apparently an effort to reduce the incentive to raise costs merely for the sake of getting price increases. Also, in cases where the profit margin limitation did apply the firm was allowed to include years ending after August 15, 1971, in calculating its base period profit margin.[70]

Perhaps the most significant change in Phase III, at

least in light of the psychological reaction with which it was greeted, was the elimination of the requirement to notify the Government in advance of price or wage increases. As the Council of Economic Advisers put it: "The program will be self-administering, in the sense that private parties can calculate the application of the standards in their own cases."[71]

Consistent with the move toward voluntary compliance, the Price Commission and the Pay Board were dissolved and their functions were transferred to the Price and Pay Divisions of the Cost of Living Council.

Rent controls, already reduced, were abolished completely. Raw food products continued to be exempt, although they were controlled after the first sale. Also, in light of the rising level of food prices, a number of steps were taken to try to increase food supplies. These included suspension of mandatory acreage set-asides for wheat, disposal of government-owned stocks of grains, termination of government loans on grain stocks, suspension of food export subsidies, and permission to graze animals on acreage diverted from crop production. However, mandatory controls were continued on food processing and distribution.[72]

The announcement of Phase III on January 11, at noon Eastern Standard time, was greeted with enthusiasm on the New York Stock Exchange. In the hour between 12:00 and 1:00 trading totaled 6,180,000 shares and the Dow-Jones Industrial Average rose from 1047.56 to 1061.14.[73] But that was the end of it. After having second thoughts, traders and investors began to fear that Phase III might mark the abandonment of the last dike against the tide of inflation. Stock prices promptly started to ease, and as of July 1974 the stock market was still below the high chalked up on January 11, 1973.

But the negative reaction to Phase III at home was as nothing compared to the reaction abroad. Against the background of a rapidly rising money supply, a burgeoning federal deficit, and what was interpreted to be the virtual abandonment of direct controls, foreigners feared the worst regarding U.S. inflation. The dollar came under intense pressure, and by February 15 a 10 percent devaluation was forced on the dollar from the Smithsonian parities established in December 1971. The dollar was then allowed to float downward, which it did into the summer of 1973 before starting upward.

The psychological reaction to Phase III revealed a latent, very strong underlying fear and expectation of continuing inflation. It must have come as a great surprise and shock to the administration. But the markets at home and abroad appeared to be right. There followed an explosion in raw commodity prices which has seldom been matched. No doubt some of this rise would have occurred in any case because of the supply shortages and strong demand conditions noted earlier. Nevertheless, the speculative fever over the expectation of continuing inflation which followed the announcement of Phase III clearly accelerated the rise.

Table 6 reveals the extent of the rise over the six-month period from December 1972 to June 1973 in farm-related commodities and industrial raw materials, compared with prices of finished goods and services. Note that the percentage increases are expressed as annual rates, i.e., percentages that would be realized if the increase for the six months should continue at the same rate for a full year. For example, the increase in the All Items Consumer Price Index was 4.0 percent for the six months, or an annual rate of 8.0 percent.

Under mounting pressure from the public and Con-

TABLE 6
Prices under Phase III

| | Index (1967 = 100) | | |
	December 1972	June 1973	Percent Increase*
Consumer Price Index			
All Items	127.3	132.4	8.0%
Food	126.0	139.8	21.9
All Items Less Food	127.6	130.3	4.2
Wholesale Price Index			
All Items	122.9	136.7	22.5
Farm Products	137.5	182.3	65.2
Finished Goods	119.5	128.7	15.4
Spot Prices—13 Industrial			
Raw Materials	134.8	170.1	52.4

*Percentage increase at annual rates.
Source: *Survey of Current Business,* November 1973, p. S-8.

gress, the administration took various steps in the late winter and spring of 1973 to retighten controls in selected areas. On March 6, major oil companies were brought under mandatory controls, including cost justification for price increases amounting to more than 1 percent per annum of revenues, and prenotification for increases greater than 1.5 percent. On March 29, ceilings were imposed on red meats at all levels of processing and distribution, though not on prices at the farm level. On May 2, prenotification requirements were imposed on firms with sales greater than $250 million proposing increases of more than 1.5 percent above levels on January 10, 1973.[74]

Finally, on June 13, a new freeze was announced covering prices but not wages. Prices were to be held at the maximum charged in the first 8 days of June. Rents were again exempted, and also raw agricultural products at the first sale. Beyond the first sale, however, raw agricultural products were subject to the ceilings. The freeze was to last for a maximum of 60 days, to be followed by new controls—Phase IV.

The food ceilings played havoc with supplies for domestic consumers. Farm products remained high under the stimulus of foreign demand and, as a result, producers and processors were squeezed between high purchase costs and frozen selling prices. Poultry and egg production declined, dramatized by news pictures of cuddly baby chicks being drowned. Supplies of red meat were similarly disrupted, offset to an extent by "custom slaughtering" on the part of some retailers. Other food processors faced like problems, particularly grain millers and fruit and vegetable canners.

PHASE IV PRICE CONTROLS

The above-noted problems in the food industry led to shortages at retail grocery stores, and resulting consumer dissatisfaction hastened the move to Phase IV. On July 18, Phase IV regulations pertaining to food were announced. They permitted a dollar-for-dollar pass-through of all farm-level price increases or decreases except for cattle, on which beef ceilings remained in effect until September 10 in order to spread out the impact of food price changes.

The Phase IV system for nonfood products became effective on August 12, 1973. In many respects it was similar to Phase II. The chief difference was that price increases could be put into effect for cost increases only on a dollar-for-dollar basis, not dollar-for-dollar plus the customary markup. Cost increases, it should be noted, were to be reduced to reflect average productivity gains in the relevant industry before being passed through to selling prices.

Firms with sales of $100 million or more per annum were required to notify the Cost of Living Council of price increases above a base level, and to wait 30 days before putting the price increase into effect, assuming the Cost of Living Council did not object within that time. Other firms were not required to prenotify the Cost of Living Council of price increases but were subject to the other rules of Phase IV. Firms with annual sales of $50 million or more were also required to file quarterly reports of prices, costs, and profits with the Cost of Living Council. Small businesses with an average of 60 or fewer employees were generally exempt from the Phase IV regulations, as they had been from the Phase II regulations.

Phase IV, in its price aspects, appears to have been designed as more of a "phase-out" than as an attempt to devise a price control system that would have any permanence. Price controls on foods were modified quickly when it became clear that they were causing shortages, notably in meats. However, keeping the lid on beef until September 10, with the idea of spreading out the post-second-freeze bulge, hardly endeared the price controllers either to the producers or to the public.

The dollar-for-dollar pass-through of cost increases was apparently aimed at handling the large jumps in the cost of purchased materials with a semblance of equity in the short run. But this kind of adjustment mechanism was bound to create disparities in price relationships which could not persist for long. By late 1973 it was becoming increasingly clear that the price controls were in fact contributing to a growing list of shortages, to which the only solution was decontrol. And so it was that the Cost of Living Council turned to phasing out individual industries from controls, extracting in return commitments of near-term restraint on price increases and promises to boost capacity. Industries so favored included lumber and plywood at the beginning of Phase IV, followed by fertilizer, cement, some metals, automobiles, tires and tubes, petrochemical feedstocks, and chemical products. Finally, on April 30 all controls were allowed to expire except those on petroleum.

In Table 7, price changes are summarized from the time of the second freeze in June 1973 to the start of Phase IV generally in August 1973, and then to April 1974, the last month of the controls. Again the changes are shown in terms of annual rates to facilitate comparisons among periods of varying lengths.

Farm product prices peaked in August 1973 and after-

TABLE 7
Prices after Phase III

	Index (1967 = 100)			Percent change*	
	June 1973	August 1973	April 1974	July-August	August-April
Consumer Price Index					
All Items	132.4	135.1	144.0	12.2%	9.9%
Food	139.8	149.4	158.6	41.2	9.2
All Items Less Food	130.3	130.9	139.7	2.8	10.1
Fuel Oil and Coal	131.6	132.8	206.5	5.5	83.2
Wholesale Price Index					
All Items	136.7	142.7	155.3	26.6	13.2
Farm Products	182.3	213.3	186.2	102.0	−19.1
Finished Goods	128.7	132.9	147.3	19.6	16.3
Petroleum Products, ref'd	146.6	145.9	288.6	−2.9	146.7
Spot Prices—13 Industrial					
Raw Materials	170.1	189.8	238.4	69.5	38.4

*Percentage change at annual rates.
Source: *Survey of Current Business*, May 1974, pp. S-8, S-9.

ward trended downward irregularly. This reflected generally improved crops abroad and the removal of restrictions on supplies in the United States, the latter leading to the prospect of rising crop production given favorable weather. Prices of finished goods and services, however, continued to rise as the increases in raw materials and petroleum worked their way through the economy.

THE BEHAVIOR OF WAGES AND SALARIES

In sharp contrast to the countless and ultimately insurmountable problems encountered with price controls, particularly from the beginning of Phase III, the wage and salary picture was marked right up to the end of controls by moderation in wage adjustments and by an absence of headline confrontations over the administration of wage and salary controls, at least from the time of the walkout by most labor representatives on the Pay Board. In particular, the 5½ percent guideline seems to have been rather widely observed in the nonunion area well into 1973. Wage adjustments in manufacturing in the nonunion area averaged 5.2 percent for 1973 as a whole, although they had risen to 6.0 percent by the fourth quarter of 1973. Even union wage adjustments in manufacturing remained at an apparently moderate 5.7 percent in 1973, the same as for 1972 and well below the 9.3 percent of 1971. It should be noted, however, that these wage changes do not include fringes.[75]

Other comparisons of more broadly based trends in compensation are shown in Table 8. This table requires careful interpretation. The average hourly compensation series includes all benefit changes, such as social security, which can at times be important, as in the first quarter

TABLE 8

Trends in Compensation (annual percentage change)

	1968	1969	1970	1971	1972	1973*	1974*
Average hourly compensation, all employees, private non-farm economy	8.2	6.4	7.1	6.8	7.0	8.1	6.6
Average hourly earnings, production workers, private non-farm economy, adjusted	6.7	6.7	6.6	6.5	6.6	6.7	5.8
Negotiated wage and benefit decisions							
First year changes	8.8	11.7	13.6	12.5	8.5	7.2	6.9
Life of contract	6.4	8.4	9.5	9.0	7.4	6.0	5.9

*First quarter annual rate.

Source: *Business Conditions Digest,* February 1972, p. 107; August 1973, p. 114; May 1974, pp. 92–93.

of 1973 when total compensation, including employer and employee contributions to social security, was up at the annual rate of 10.8 percent. The index of average hourly earnings does not include benefits but is adjusted to eliminate the effects of overtime and shifts between higher-paying and lower-paying industries. The lack of such an adjustment in the average hourly compensation series is likely responsible for the drop in that series in the first quarter of 1974. Negotiated wage and benefit decisions do not include the effect of cost-of-living adjustment provisions.

Unsatisfactory as any one of the series in Table 8 may be as an ideal measure of general wage and salary trends, taken as a whole they reveal a remarkable moderation in wage changes in view of the substantial increase of prices in 1973, particularly for food. Real spendable earnings, after taxes and adjusted for price increases, declined through most of 1973. We can't help but observe, however, that increases of even the amounts shown are not compatible with stability of prices because they still exceed substantially the gain in productivity that can be expected as a long-run matter.

The disparate behavior between price and compensation changes is of the utmost significance, especially in light of the general tendency to speak of "wage *and* price" controls in one breath. They should be separated. All of the economic difficulties with controls have come in the *price* area, notably where excess demand in relation to limited supplies at the controlled price created disruptions of supply channels, such as diversion to the export market, and inefficiencies in acquiring supplies that were available, as typified by the long lines at gas stations in the winter of 1973–74. These demonstrate effectively that price controls just will not work where demands substantially exceed supplies at the fixed prices.

But the controls on compensation occasioned no comparable problems. I have not heard of one case where the limitation of compensation changes caused a widespread shortage of some badly needed skill, though there must have been at least one somewhere. This experience indicates that controls, where supply exceeds demand at the controlled price, as is generally true in the labor market as a whole, may have a useful role to play.

EVALUATION

Our evaluation of the U.S. experiment in direct controls is made with the object of determining the contribution controls can make to a permanent system of institutions which will promote maximum employment with minimum inflation. At this point, once again, we want to make it clear that we believe monetary and fiscal policies have the major role to play in attaining this objective. But the general outlines of such policies are known, and we will not attempt to elaborate on them here. It is our conviction that appropriate monetary and fiscal policies are necessary but not sufficient conditions for achieving full employment without inflation. Our analysis has pointed to the likelihood that in the absence of some direct controls inflation will proceed almost, but not quite, irrespective of the rate of employment or unemployment, given our present institutions relating to the settling of wage bargains and the commitment to full employment.

At first blush, it is difficult to see how one can be encouraged by the results under the controls. Although prices did slow in their rise through 1972, over the period from the freeze in August 1971 to April 1974 the Consumer Price Index rose 17.9 percent, an average annual rate of 6.7 percent. Moreover, the annual rate of rise reached 11.1 percent for the six months ended April 1974. Behavior of the Wholesale Price Index was even worse. Although this index declined slightly immediately following the freeze, it rose 36.1 percent from August 1971 to April 1974, an average rate of 13.5 percent per annum. For the six months ended April 1974 the rise was at the rate of 22.7 percent per annum. Surely this is proof enough of the failure of the controls system.

But this is to look at the question of success or failure of the controls from the very narrow and incorrect view merely of their ability to control particular prices and the price level in general. For it is our conclusion that there is just no substitute for the market price system as an organizer of economic activity. Interference with the free movement of prices is bound to lead to shortages and to misallocation of resources so that as a nation we do not produce the maximum satisfaction or real income possible with our resources.

This general proposition was illustrated in numerous specific instances under the controls: lumber; chickens; meat products generally under the 1973 freeze, but particularly beef; and fertilizer, cement and some lines of paper among industrial commodities, to name only those which attracted public attention. The whole energy crisis is perhaps an even more vivid illustration of the perverse impact of controls, starting years ago with the regulation of the price of natural gas moving interstate and probably with additional problems still to come.

Thus it can perhaps be considered a benefit if out of the experience with controls a consensus should emerge that *price* controls should form no part of a permanent arsenal of antiinflation weapons. Not only have such controls not stopped the rise of the general level of prices, they have done positive harm in at least the individual instances cited above. Moreover, the controls do not seem to have brought about any material lessening of the expectation of continuing inflation which was the Nixon economists' hope and their main rationalization for the imposition of price controls in the first place. The explosive rise of prices and flight from the dollar following the announcement of Phase III proved that the expectation of continuing inflation is not something that can be eroded with the cosmetic of price controls.

It may be unfortunate in some ways that the controls

program had to weather two pervasive situations of actual shortage—actual in the sense of an absolute decrease of supply, first in the case of food products and later in petroleum. The situation was further confounded by the devaluations of the dollar which raised the cost of imports, particularly raw materials and hence domestic products made from them. Also, to the extent that the devaluations brought about a positive shift in the balance of payments for goods and services—and net exports went from an annual rate of $1.1 billion in the third quarter of 1971 to $12.8 billion in the fourth quarter of 1973—this also contributed to a shrinkage in the supply of goods and services that might otherwise have been available to the domestic market.

Thus, with an absolute shrinkage in important segments of total supplies in the domestic market, it was inevitable that prices would rise on average relative to incomes, as happened. The growth of real income per person stagnated in 1973 because we could not eat or otherwise use supplies which were shipped abroad or not produced. In the longer run, however, we can expect that advancing output per person will lead to a rise in money incomes relative to prices so that the real standard of living will increase.

It is therefore of the utmost importance that money incomes be restrained from chasing the higher price level. Prices had to rise relative to money incomes to achieve a reduction in real demand commensurate with the relative decline in supplies available to consumers. An attempt to offset price increases by raising money incomes will be frustrated for the economy as a whole in the absence of increasing supplies, though it is possible

202

for individuals and for some groups to shift the burden of adjustment to others if they succeed in raising their own incomes, and if this is not emulated by others.

It is therefore encouraging that compensation increases did not rise appreciably as the price level bulged in 1973. Particularly encouraging was the behavior of wage and salary adjustments in the nonunion sector. Not only was the rate of increase within the 5½ percent guideline, but this was apparently accomplished without creating the kinds of shortages which attracted so much attention in the markets for products. It reinforces our judgment that for the nonorganized sector of the market for wage and salary earners it should be possible to work down to low rates of unemployment without precipitating an inflationary spiral—in the absence of influence from the union side, of course.

It is also encouraging—if somewhat surprising—that settlements in the union area have also moderated from the pace of earlier settlements, such as those of 1970 and 1971 before the freeze. In addition to patriotic restraint on the part of individual unions, credit for the progress thus far must be given to the guidelines in general and to the Construction Industry Stabilization Committee, the Pay Board, and the Cost of Living Council in particular. It is imperative that this degree of restraint in the .union area be continued and, if possible, carried still further to gradually cool down the inflationary climate.

There remains one very unfortunate feature of the control system. This is the tendency to tie price and wage controls together. There seems to be a feeling that it would be politically impossible to have pay control without price control.

This can only mean that there is a widespread lack of

understanding about the relationships among pay, prices and profits—a belief that somehow they are divorced from one another in general, and in particular that if pay is held down, prices can rise independently and profits will run away. While this can be true for individual products, industries, or even small countries in a world market, and while it is *theoretically* possible even more broadly, the fact remains that under conditions encountered in practice in the United States, and in the domestic industries of other countries, prices, pay and profits have always been closely related in the past and are likely to be in the future. It is therefore imperative that pay be restrained to hold down the general price level while individual prices are free to fluctuate relative to each other.

Again, we hasten to emphasize that this does not mean that we can rely exclusively on direct controls of compensation and other forms of income. As with product prices, the economy is just too complicated for this. In time, distortions would be created in the markets for persons in the same way as with price controls for products. Therefore, it is necessary to rely primarily on monetary and fiscal policies to keep overall demand rising only in step with the rise in production, and no more, if the price level is to be kept under control.

But while controlling overall demand is a necessary condition for inflation control, it is not sufficient. For even with demand kept under control, both theoretical reasoning and practical experience indicate that cost-push inflation will take place in portions of the economy where collective bargaining is virtually marketwise in scope. Therefore, some form of direct restraint is needed in key collective bargaining settlements. Otherwise there is danger that negotiated settlements will run higher than the guideline and become a standard to which the rest of the economy must adjust if reasonably full employment is to be attained.

The need for flexibility in wage setting if the labor market is to operate efficiently means that the great bulk of wage decisions must be decontrolled from the pay standards. Where collective bargaining does not operate, or where there is effective competition between union and nonunion firms, one can rely on straight demand control to keep the rise in income within bounds, and still allow flexibility to meet changes in relative demands and in the relative supplies of different occupations and skills. However, where rates of pay are not effectively restrained by direct competition in the labor market, as they are not with marketwide collective bargaining, then direct restraint is required to see that settlements do not exceed the guideposts.

9

Conclusion: The Road Ahead

NOW let us first recapitulate and then conclude with a statement of the policies needed to achieve full employment without inflation in the years ahead.

The skeleton of our underlying argument can be summarized in 10 points:

1. At acceptable levels of employment, i.e., with employment over 95 percent of the labor force, prices tend to rise in unpredictable fashion.

2. Prices tend to rise in unpredictable fashion as a result of the market structure under which collective bargaining takes place. Specifically, where pay rates negotiated in collective bargaining settlements are generalized to all firms in a market, there is small incentive for any one firm to resist the demands of a union, particularly if the union represents a small segment of the total labor force, such as pipefitters in construction or teamsters in food distribution.

3. Settlements reached in one area tend to become the standard for settlements in other areas and the means by which the whole pay system is ratcheted upward, given the commitment to full employment.

4. In the area of effective competition in the labor market this sort of ratcheting is not likely to take place. Given such effective competition, income restraint can be maintained in the nonunion area by controlling demand through monetary and fiscal policy, particularly by maintaining a steady, moderate rate of expansion in the money stock.

5. Part of the reason for excessive union demands is the feeling that raising wage rates will increase the share of output going to wages and salaries as against profits. This apparently is fostered by a public attitude favoring a more equal distribution of income.

6. However, there is a relationship which appears to be relatively fixed in the long run between prices and employment costs per unit (the latter affected by pay rates and productivity). This relationship varies with the state of business conditions and does not hold for individual firms or groups of firms. But it does hold over time for the economy as a whole in this country and for the domestic industries of foreign countries.

7. Therefore, increases in labor costs are bound in the long run to be reflected proportionately in higher prices and not in an increase in the share of income going to wages and salaries. Efforts to improve the lot of labor should therefore be directed at increasing the economic capacity of individuals through education, training, and increasing the supply of capital. Efforts to increase the equality of income distribution should be aimed at the system of taxes and transfer payments.

8. The price system is essential to organize modern

economies to satisfy effectively the diversity of wants of
the consumer, particularly as the number of choices open
to consumers and producers expands geometrically over
time. This requires flexibility of prices and wages and
salaries so that changes in demand and supply conditions
can be reflected in profits, which in turn will signal and
motivate particular lines of activity to expand or contract.
We rely on the profit potential to allocate existing resources to the production of goods and services consumers want most, to stimulate the search for new products
and technology, to improve existing products and technology, and to serve as a source of funds for capital
investment. To some extent these functions may conflict
with the apparent desire for a more equal distribution
of income.

9. One possible solution for the tendency of wage
costs and prices to rise unpredictably in modern economies would be to abolish marketwide collective bargaining. However, given the widespread presence of labor
unions of varying degrees of power in all modern ad-
vanced nations, such a solution seems visionary.

10. Therefore, any control system that is to be viable
over time must allow for flexibility in the price system
and at the same time provide for direct limitation on the
wage bargains reached in marketwide collective bargaining. Any other system would break down because distortions and shortages would gradually develop in the pattern of production or, in the absence of direct controls
on wage bargains in pattern-setting industries, it would
result in inflation.

THE VOICE OF EXPERIENCE

The system of direct controls in the United States from
August 1971 through April 1974 demonstrates that di-

rect control of prices, *particularly of items where demand exceeds supply at the controlled price,* leads to intolerable shortages of supply and disruptions in the distribution of supplies available. As a nation, we must face the fact that we cannot raise our standard of living by holding down prices. Our standard of living is governed by our ability to produce, and recent experience demonstrates that a free price system is the only practical mechanism for seeing to it that our productive capacity is allocated to produce the things consumers want most.

On the other hand, experience with wage and salary controls, as distinct from price controls, suggests that they did play a role in bringing down the rise in compensation during the control period, and without creating noticeable widespread shortages of particular abilities and skills such as occurred in product markets under price controls. Nevertheless, one can imagine that such shortages and disruptions would likely occur in time if the relationships among wages and salaries were frozen for an extended period.

The average of prices of goods and services has been closely related to labor costs over the years, and there is no reason to believe that the relationship will be different in the future. Therefore, if labor costs are held down, prices will also be held down. Wages and salaries are not only the principal element in total costs but are also the principal source for spending.

To reach the ultimate goal of reducing the rate of price inflation to zero would require that the rise in wage and salary costs per unit of output should also be reduced to zero. This means that wages and salaries could increase no more rapidly than production of goods and services. The increase in production in the private economy has averaged less than 3 percent annually per hour of work in recent years. Hence 3 percent per annum per hour of work is the maximum increase in wages and salaries that would be compatible with a tolerable approach to stability of the price level.

It would be impractical, however, to try to reach immediately a standard increase of 3 percent per annum in total compensation costs, including fringes, per hour of work. This is because many existing contracts cover more than one year and are in different stages of catchup to past inflation, and the latter is also true in the nonunion segment of the working population. Therefore, the objective can only be reached gradually.

The standard guideline for any one year might be 3 percent plus half the increase in the Consumer Price Index in the preceding year. For example, if the Consumer Price Index should be up 10 percent for 1974, the 1975 guideline could be half of this, 5 percent, plus 3 percent for productivity growth, or 8 percent in total. If prices should rise 8 percent in 1975, the 1976 guideline could be half of this plus 3 percent, a total of 7 percent. Thereafter the guideline might be reduced by one half point per year until the 3 percent figure is reached. Experience might indicate that this schedule could be speeded up, but it is best to have modest expectations at the start and to stick to them, again with recent experience in mind.

RECOMMENDATIONS FOR ACTION—THE INCOME SETTLEMENTS BOARD (ISB)

Experience in the United States and Europe teaches that implementation of the suggested guideline policy cannot be left to hortatory appeals alone (i.e., to "jaw-boning"). Backing by the force of law is needed. Experience, particularly in Britain, also points to the desirability of having the cooperation of organized labor in carrying out an incomes policy.

It is therefore recommended that a permanent board, to be called The Income Settlements Board, or ISB, be established under the President by act of Congress. To keep the number of members manageable, the ISB should consist of eight persons, of whom four would be from organized labor and four from the general public. They might serve staggered terms of four years to permit rotation. One of the four labor representatives should be appointed Chairman.

The reason for the heavy preponderance of labor representatives is that the functions of the Board would relate to collective bargaining settlements. Its specific duties should be to:

1. Set the standard wage and salary increase for the current year each January on the basis of the latest available information. This should be in accordance with the formula set forth above; the Board should have no discretion in this.
2. Publicize the standard and urge that it be followed wherever possible in nonunion as well as union areas (the "jawbone").
3. Require that all collective bargaining contracts providing increases above the guideline in compensation plus fringes be submitted to the Board for approval or modification. Penalties should be imposed on employers for violations of this requirement as a practical means of enforcement.
4. Develop standards for approving increases beyond

the guidelines, a necessity to cover "inequities" in the early stages. Such approvals will need to be held to a minimum if the guideline is to be approached as a general average. However, it can be expected that many increases will fall below the guideline, as they did in the United States under Phases II through IV, which will leave room for some above-guideline increases. The latter must be severely limited to cases of demonstrated shortages of skills and the most egregious inequities. Experience with price controls demonstrates that it is counterproductive to try to maintain a ceiling on an item (or skill) in short supply at the fixed price.

A key point in the foregoing program is the support of organized labor, which to some may seem unrealistically visionary. Yet, if this program is to have support in any case, it will require that the public in general, and thought leaders in particular, face the facts realistically. We believe the public is anxious to do this and is looking for guidance from knowledgeable leaders. It is hoped that the leaders of organized labor will see and accept the logic, facts, and experience underlying the recommendations made here and will support them in the interest of promoting the welfare of labor in particular and the public in general. If they decline to participate, as with the Pay Board in the United States, it is reluctantly recommended that the Board be created in any case, but that it consist of seven public members, with the powers and duties outlined previously.

THE TIP ALTERNATIVE

Our analysis of the nature of the inflation-prone bias in our economy has highlighted marketwide collective bargaining as the key point in the problem. With market-wide collective bargaining, the employer's incentive to resist union demands is reduced substantially compared with what his resistance would be in a competitive labor market. We have suggested, therefore, that direct restraint is needed on such settlements. Others, making essentially the same diagnosis, prescribe a less direct approach to stiffening the backs of employers in wage negotiations. In particular, Henry Wallich, formerly of Yale University and now a member of the Board of Governors of the Federal Reserve System, and Sidney Weintraub of the University of Pennsylvania, have proposed using the corporate income tax for this purpose, a proposal they call a Tax-Based Incomes Policy, or TIP.[76]

The Wallich-Weintraub proposal would "backbone" employers in wage negotiations by levying a surcharge on the income tax of corporations granting wage increases in excess of the wage guideline. The surcharge would be in addition to the present normal-plus-surtax of 48 percent and would be proportional to the excess of wage increases above the guideline, with a tapering feature for high increases so that the tax would not wipe out profits completely and hence destroy incentives. As with our proposal, Wallich and Weintraub look upon their scheme as a supplement to and not as a substitute for appropriate monetary and fiscal policies.

There are several reasons why we believe their proposal to be a less desirable way to attack the problem. Some of the difficulties are recognized by the authors themselves in the references cited. One is a question as to whether the tax would be shifted to consumers. In the case of public utilities and possibly in some other areas it might be, though we are inclined to agree with the authors that in most cases the tax would not be shifted, particularly in the short run. However, this is still a matter of debate among economists. To the extent that the tax could be shifted its effectiveness as a backbone strengthener would be reduced.

A second problem involves the statistical difficulty of measuring wage increases and benefits and relating them to a base. This would be a problem also with the direct regulation of negotiated settlements. However, in our judgment it would be less of a problem where the measurement is to be applied only to those collective bargaining settlements which may exceed the guideline, than where it must be applied against all wage (and salary?) adjustments for all corporations with profits above a given figure (they suggest $1 million).

A final criticism relates to the fact that their proposed penalty applies only to corporations, whereas the problem to be attacked is related to the structure of bargaining in particular labor markets and only by chance to whether the employer is organized as a corporation or not. As they point out themselves, their proposal may not get at the problems in construction and trucking, which may require direct restraint in any case. There are also questions of this sort regarding governmental and not-for-profit enterprises.

We believe that in this stage in the history of our approach to controlling inflation, a direct restraint on settlements is more likely to bring about the necessary decline in increases than is the TIP proposal. Also, direct controls on collective bargaining settlements, plus a "jawbone" on the need for overall restraint in income increases, would allow a greater degree of flexibility in adjusting relative wages and salaries than would likely be true with the surcharge. Again, the surcharge would apply to all corporations with profits above the minimum profit cutoff, which would tend to freeze wage and salary relationships at their base period structure. The ISB approach would allow some flexibility within collective bargaining settlements but would leave noncollective-bargaining adjustments free to fluctuate and of course would not apply to collective bargaining settlements at or below the guideline.

ISB A SUPPLEMENT—NOT A SUBSTITUTE

We conclude with one final reiteration—that the direct control proposed for collective bargaining settlements is a necessary but not a sufficient condition for halting inflation. Monetary-fiscal policy will still be needed; in fact, it will be more critical than ever. While this book does not go into the criteria for setting appropriate monetary-fiscal policy, since that is another story which is presumably well known already, a few concluding words on the relationship of incomes policy to monetary-fiscal policy may be in order.

Experience in the United States and abroad illustrates that controls under conditions of excess demand just will not work. And the greater the excess demand over available supplies at the price fixed, the more damage will a particular control do in disrupting supplies and channels of distribution while it lasts, and the more certain it is to break down in time. Consequently, we cannot rely on price controls to prevent inflation but must rely on indirect control of overall demand through monetary and fiscal policy plus the direct restraint of incomes that might otherwise rise in a manner inappropriate to keeping the average level of product prices in line.

The reason direct control is needed in addition to monetary-fiscal restraint is that, again as experience demonstrates, income settlements growing out of collective bargaining across market lines will escalate beyond the guideline in the absence of direct control, to a large extent irrespective of demand conditions and hence independent, to a large extent again, of the level of unemployment in the economy generally or in the particular line affected. Given the commitment to high employment, and a general stickiness of wage and salary rates downward, the beyond-guideline settlements tend to become generalized by making it necessary to allow the economy to inflate if excessive unemployment is to be avoided. Restrictive monetary-fiscal policy becomes impractical, except for brief interludes, and inflation proceeds.

With collective bargaining settlements held directly to the guideline or below, and with product prices and other wages and salaries free to move, a very special burden will be placed on monetary-fiscal policy to keep the overall level of demand increasing at roughly the proper rate to allow wages and salaries in the noncontrolled sector to rise at approximately the guideline rate. If monetary-fiscal policy is appropriate in this sense, it will furnish sufficient buying power to keep prices rising in the zone of the targeted rate (ultimately zero) but not more.

Some slippage from absolute targets must be tolerated in practice, as indicated by my use of the words "roughly," "approximately," and "in the zone of." But the slippage must be limited, and policy should lean in the direction of under- rather than over-stimulation. If monetary-fiscal policy should fall short of the proper degree of monetary-fiscal expansion, it would cause average prices and incomes to fall below the target, which would create an inequity in the noncontrolled sector relative to the controlled sector. More dangerous to continued stability, however, would be an excessive degree of monetary-fiscal stimulus; this would cause average incomes to exceed the target, raising costs and creating buying power in excess of amounts compatible with the price guideline. If the target should continue to be missed on the high side, the wage guideline would also break down in due course, as a matter of equity if not of demand pull.

To repeat once more for absolute clarity, controls will not work where there is excess *demand* at the fixed price, wage, or salary. They will work only where there is excess *supply* at the fixed price, i.e., in the case of wages, if there is unemployment (hopefully a minimum) at the wage fixed. With excess supply at the price or wage fixed, controls serve the function of preventing the whole market supply function from being shifted upward.[77]

The appropriateness of monetary-fiscal policy is therefore at least as crucial in the overall policy mix when it is combined with incomes policy as when it is acting alone. For monetary-fiscal policy, by itself, cannot prevent inflation in any case—short of an intolerably long period of years at unacceptable levels of unemployment. So mistakes are not so critical. We hasten to add that incomes policy cannot succeed by itself either. The two must be combined if we are to bring inflation down; and they must be coordinated and skillfully executed to achieve agreed-upon targets. With such a coordinated, mutually reinforcing combination of fiscal-monetary and incomes policies, we can look forward with confident hope to halting inflation and still keeping our jobs. In fact, we should be able to achieve a higher rate of employment of the labor force than in the postwar years. We should be satisfied with nothing less than reducing unemployment to 3 percent and price inflation to zero.

Notes

1. Public Law 304, 79th Congress.

2. U.S. Department of Commerce. *Business Conditions Digest,* June 1972, p. 107.

3. S. Lebergott. *Manpower in Economic Growth: The American Record Since 1800.* New York: McGraw-Hill, 1964, Appendix Table A-3, p. 512.

4. James Tobin. "Inflation and Unemployment." *The American Economic Review,* vol. LXII, March 1972, p. 9.

5. *Business Conditions Digest,* op. cit., pp. 75 and 90.

6. A. W. Phillips. "The Relation Between Unemployment and the Rate of Change of Money Wage Rates in the United Kingdom: 1861–1957." *Economica,* New Series, vol. XXV, no. 100: November 1958, pp. 283–299.

7. Otto Eckstein and Roger Brinner, *The Inflation Process in the United States.* Joint Economic Committee, Congress of the United States. Washington: U.S. Government Printing Office, 1972, p. 5.

8. *Economic Report of The President,* January 1962, pp. 46–49.

9. Eckstein and Brinner, op. cit., p. 40.

10. Milton Friedman. "The Role of Monetary Policy." *The American Economic Review,* vol. LVIII, March 1968, p. 8.

11. Ibid., p. 10.

12. Ibid., p. 11.

13. *Economic Report of The President,* January 1972, p. 115.

14. Lebergott, op. cit., p. 524.

15. Statement of John M. Blair, Chief Economist for the Subcommittee, before the Subcommittee on Antitrust and Monopoly of the Committee on the Judiciary, United States Senate, *Hearings on Economic Concentration,* 89th Congress, Part 5, September 12, 1966, p. 1891.

16. *Fortune,* vol. LXXXV, May 1972, no. 5, pp. 184–185.

17. Statement of John M. Blair, op. cit., p. 1892.

18. *Economic Report of The President,* January 1972, pp. 195 and 280.

19. *Economic Indicators,* March 1974.

20. 38 Stat. 731 (1914), as reproduced in Heinrick Kronstein, John T. Miller, Jr., Paul P. Dommer. *Major American Antitrust Laws.* Washington, D.C.: Institute for International and Foreign Trade Law, Georgetown University, 1965, p. 403.

21. *Statistical Abstract of the United States.*

22. *Labor Unions in the United States.* Washington, D.C.: U.S. Department of Labor, Bureau of Labor Statistics, 1970, Bulletin 1665, 1970, p. 67.

23. *Labor Union and Employee Association Membership.* Washington, D.C.: U.S. Department of Labor, Bureau of Labor Statistics, release dated 9/13/71.

24. "The New Conservatism." *Time Magazine,* November 26, 1956.

25. Lebergott, op. cit., p. 160.

26. H. Gregg Lewis. *Unionism and Relative Wages in the United States.* Chicago: The University of Chicago Press, 1963, p. 193.

27. Ibid., p. 187.

28. L. W. Weiss. "Concentration and Labor Earnings." *The American Economic Review,* vol. 56, March 1966, p. 115.

29. *Economic Report of The President,* February 1970, p. 62.

30. Ibid., p. 63.

31. *Economic Report of The President,* January 1972, p. 66.

32. Ibid., p. 108

33. *Survey of Current Business,* April 1974, pp. 13–14.

34. Recollection from class notes, *circa* 1940.

35. *Economic Report of The President,* January 1962, p. 174.

36. Ibid., p. 183.

37. Ibid., p. 185.

38. Ibid., p. 189.

39. *Economic Report of The President,* January 1964, p. 115.

40. *Economic Report of The President,* January 1966, p. 92.

41. Ibid., p. 87.

42. John Sheahan, *The Wage-Price Guideposts.* Washington, D.C.: The Brookings Institution, 1967, p. 79.

43. See also George P. Shultz and Robert Z. Aliber, editors, *Guidelines, Informal Controls and The Market Place.* Chicago: The University of Chicago Press, 1966, especially Part I, pp. 1–80.

45. R. G. Lipsey. "The Relationship Between Unemployment and the Rate of Change of Money Wage Rates in the U.K., 1862–1957." *Economica,* vol. 27, Feb. 1960, pp. 1–31.

45. John Sheahan, op. cit., p. 81.

46. J. Murray Edelman and R. W. Fleming. *The Politics of Wage-Price Decisions.* Urbana: University of Illinois Press, 1965, p. 153.

47. Ibid., p. 219.

48. E. H. Phelps Brown. "Guidelines for Growth and for Incomes in the United Kingdom: Some Possible Lessons for the United States," in George P. Shultz and Robert Z. Aliber, editors, *Guidelines, Informal Controls, and The Market Place,* Chicago: The University of Chicago Press. 1966, pp. 144–145.

49. Lloyd Ulman and Robert J. Flanagan. *Wage Restraint: A Study of Incomes Policies in Western Europe.* Berkeley: University of California Press, 1971, p. 66.

50. Ibid., pp. 90–91.

51. Odd Aukrust, "Prim I: A Model of the Price and Income Distribution Mechanism of an Open Economy." *Artikler Fra Statistisk Sentralbyra No. 35,* 1970, p. 9, note 1.

52. Ibid., p. 38.

53. Gosta Edgren, Karl-Olof Faxen, and Clas-Erik Odhner. "Wages, Growth and the Distribution of Income." *The Swedish Journal of Economics,* 1969, p. 138.

54. Ibid., p. 146.

55. Ibid., p. 138.

56. Ibid., p. 149.

57. Ulman and Flanagan, op. cit., p. 95.

58. Ibid., pp. 132–134.

59. Ibid., p. 163.

60. *Economic Report of The President,* January 1973, p. 57.

61. Ibid., p. 60.

62. Ibid., p. 62.

63. Ibid., pp. 62–64.

64. Edgar R. Fiedler. "The Case Against Rigid Controls." *The Wall Street Journal,* April 19, 1973.

65. *Economic Indicators,* May 1974, p. 29.

66. *Federal Budget Trends.* St. Louis: Federal Reserve Bank of St. Louis, May 9, 1974, p. 2.

67. Statement of Dr. John T. Dunlop, Director, Cost of Living Council, Before the Subcommittee on Production and Stabilization of the Senate Committee on Banking, Housing and Urban Affairs, February 6, 1974, Appendix A, p. A-1.

68. *Economic Report of The President,* February 1974, p. 222.

69. *Business Conditions Digest,* May 1974, p. 80.

70. *Economic Report of The President,* January 1973, p. 82.

71. Ibid., p. 81.

72. Ibid., p. 79.

222

73. *Barron's,* January 15, 1973, p. 62.

74. *Economic Report of The President,* January 1974, pp. 94–99, and Statement of John T. Dunlop, op. cit., pp. A-19–21, for this and following material through Phase IV.

75. *Current Wage Developments.* Washington, D.C.: U.S. Department of Labor, February 1973, Table 7.

76. Henry Wallich, *Newsweek,* September 5, 1966 and December 14, 1970. *The New York Times,* December 16, 1970. Sidney Weintraub, "An Incomes Policy to Stop Inflation," *Lloyds Bank Review,* January 1970 and "Proposal to Halt the Spiral of Wages and Prices," *The New York Times,* November 29, 1970. Wallich and Weintraub, "A Tax-Based Incomes Policy," *Journal of Economic Issues,* June 1971, pp. 1–13. Also discussion in *Journal of Economic Issues,* December 1972.

77. I would like to express my appreciation to Abba P. Lerner, Queens College, City University of New York, for clarifying this notion and for planting many other stimulating thoughts over the years.

Index

Blair, John M., 48
Board of Government Mediators
(Netherlands), 137
Boldt, George H., 175
Bookkeeper, wage adjustments for,
65–66, 73, 91
Boom excesses, 2–3
Brinner, Roger, 12, 16
British Employers' Confederation
(BEC), 123
Brown, E. H. Phelps, 131
Building industry
decline in demand as affecting
wage settlements, 79
employers' capitulation to unions'
demands, 74–78
employment in, 24–25
minority of employees extorting
higher wages, 101–2
outsize wage demand settlement,
77
teamsters' settlements, 78
unemployment rate, 76–77
wage adjustments, 76
Built-in stabilizers, adoption of, 3
Business, public attitude toward,
6–7
Business cycles
lessening of, 46
price-labor costs relationship
changes, 56–58

C

Capital per person, increase in, 59
Capital resources as source of prof-
its, 39–40
Catholic Workers Union (KEV)
(Netherlands), 136
Central Bureau of Statistics of Nor-
way, 145
Central Planning Bureau (Nether-
lands), 137
Civilian labor force, 23
unemployment percent, 45
Clayton Act, 55
Coal industry, 135
Collective bargaining, 8; see also La-
bor unions

Collective bargaining—*Cont.*
controls on operation of, 102
inflationary wage-price spiral,
cause of, 73
limitation on union's right of,
105–6
marketwide basis, 72–80, 95–96,
100–101, 203
abolition of, 207
limitation upon, 207
restraint on, need for, 211–12,
214
Company-wide union settlements,
limitation to, 98–99
Competition
foreign, 49
growth of, 38
interproduct, 49
labor markets, introduction into,
86–103
Competitive labor market defined,
98
Concentration among individual industries, 48
higher earnings in, basis for,
82–83
Confederation of Swedish Trade
Unions (LO), 145
Confindustria (Italy), 161
Conglomeration, 48
Construction industry; see Building
industry
Construction Industry Stabilization
Commission, 176
Construction Industry Stabilization
Committee, 76, 202
Consumer
free choice in price system,
28–29, 38, 86–88
victimization for profits, 28
Consumer Price Index, 7, 117, 180,
191–92, 195, 199, 209
1920s, 47
upward bias, 22
Contract construction industry; see
Building industry
Controls, 7; see also Wage and price
control system *and* Wage and
price controls

Economic Report—Cont.
  (1966), 116–17
  (1967), 117
  (1972), 104
  (1973), 180
Economic Report of the President, 23
Economic Stabilization Act of 1970,
  177–78
Edelman, J. Murray, 122 n
Electricity, monopoly situation in,
  88–89
Employee compensation, 51, 54
Employers
  alternative to hire union or
    nonunion labor, 98
  backboning in wage negotiations,
    212
  capitulation to union demands,
    70–78, 93–97
  duty to resist union demands, 114
Employment
  full; *see* Full employment
  overseas levels of opportunity, 4
  stability, 3
Employment Act of 1946, 1–2, 7, 9,
  44
Energy controls, 183
Energy crisis, 200
England; *see* United Kingdom
Equilibrium situation, 91
European wage-price controls; *see*
  Incomes policy *and specific na-
  tions*
Excess profits tax, 108
Executive, choice to become, 29–
  30, 35
Expansion in economy, 1967–1968,
  15
Export-import costs, increase in,
  187
Export industries (Norway and
  Sweden), 147–51
Externalities, 36–37

F

Fair Labor Standards Act, 177
Farm product prices, 182, 195–96
Farming advances, 89

Fast-food franchise, 32–34
Federal Reserve Bank of Cleveland,
  119
Federal Reserve Board
  discount rate raised by, 15
  Index of Industrial Production,
    56
  monetary policy, 3
Federal reserves, sensitivity to economic changes, 3
Federation of British Industries,
  123, 127–28
Finance industries, employment in,
  24–25
Finished goods and services prices,
  195–96
Fiscal policy; *see* Monetary and fiscal
  policy
Fixed incomes, rising prices as dis-
  crimination against, 5
Flanagan, Robert J., 122 n, 153
Fleming, R. W., 122 n
Floating exchange rates, adjustment
  to, 188
Food
  ceilings, 192–93
  chain in large metropolitan area,
    wage adjustments in, 68–72
  export subsidies, suspension of,
    190
  industry problems, 193
  processing and distribution, con-
    trols on, 190
  supplies
    increase in, 190
    shortages, 201
Footnotes, 218–22
Foreign competition, 49
Foreign demand, rise in, 182
Foreign trade, dependence on, 153
Fortune, 48
Foundation of Labor (Netherlands),
  136–37
Frame wage agreements (Norway
  and Sweden), 145
France, 123
  incomes policy, 156–58
    central planning, high degree
      of, 156–57

228

232

Norway and Sweden incomes policy—*Cont.*
Confederation of Swedish Trade Unions, 145
economic forecasts by government, 145
evaluation, 151–53
export industries, 147–51
exposed industries, 147–48, 150
foreign developments, effect of, 151
"frame" wage agreements, 145
international economic influences, 145–47
low-paid workers, 152–53
price freeze, 151
sheltered industries, 147–48, 151
strong labor-employer organizations, 144–45
Swedish Central Organization of Salaried Employees, 149
Swedish Confederation of Trade Unions, 149
Swedish Employers' Confederation, 144, 149
Swedish version, 148–51
wage bargaining, 150
NRA Codes, 165–66

O–P

Oil companies, controls on, 192
Patents as legal monopolies, 89
Pay Board, 175–77, 180, 190, 196, 202
Pay pause for government workers (United Kingdom), 124–25
Pay standards under New Economic Policy; *see* New Economic Policy
Permissive wage increases, 114
Petroleum controls, 195
Petroleum prices, 196
Petroleum refining industry, 182
Petroleum shortage, 201
Phase-out period of controls, 183, 194–95
Phase II of New Economic Policy, 175–77, 180–83

Phase III of New Economic Policy, 183, 189–93
Phase IV of New Economic Policy, 183, 193–98
Phillips, A. W., 10
Phillips curve, 9–26; *see also* Unemployment
critical unemployment rate, 17
defined, 10
Eckstein-Brinner version, 12–13, 16, 20–21, 119
expression of, 10–11
Friedmanesque, 60
lags in price change-employment change relationship, 15, 61
long-run, 13–17, 60
natural rate of unemployment, 17; *see also* Natural rate of unemployment
nonunion workers, 61–62
short-run, 14, 61
trade-off between unemployment and inflation, 9–10
uncertainty, element of, 15–17
union workers, 61–62
United Kingdom, 10–12
United States, 11–15
vertical, 17, 21, 60
wage adjustments in nonunion sector, 67
wage-price guideposts, shift during period of, 118
Photography industry, advances in, 89
Plasterers, wage demands of, 75–76
Plumber, choice to become, 35
Pollution problems, 36–37
Postwar period, 1–3
inflationary environment, 46
market system, 3–4
profit squeeze, 53
unemployment rate, 45
Power, defined, 64
Price
changes in, wage changes in relation to, 10–11
control of, 7; *see also* Price controls
flexibility in system of, 207
increase target, 22